D1301445

WHAT IS TRANSPARENCY?

RICHARD W. OLIVER

McGraw-Hill

New York   Chicago   San Francisco   Lisbon
London   Madrid   Mexico City   Milan   New Delhi
San Juan   Seoul   Singapore   Sydney   Toronto

DISCARDED

BOWLING GREEN STATE
UNIVERSITY LIBRARIES

The McGraw·Hill Companies

Copyright © 2004 by The McGraw-Hill Companies, Inc. All rights reserved. Printed in the United States of America. Except as permitted under the United States Copyright Act of 1976, no part of this publication may be reproduced or distributed in any form or by any means, or stored in a data base or retrieval system, without the prior written permission of the publisher.

1 2 3 4 5 6 7 8 9 0   AGM/AGM   0 9 8 7 6 5 4

ISBN 0-07-143548-4

McGraw-Hill books are available at special quantity discounts to use as premiums and sales promotions, or for use in corporate training programs. For more information, please write to the Director of Special Sales, McGraw-Hill Professional, Two Penn Plaza, New York, NY 10121-2298. Or contact your local bookstore.

Library of Congress Cataloging-in-Publication Data.

Oliver, Richard W.
    What is transparency? / by Richard W. Oliver.—1st ed.
        p.   cm.
    ISBN 0-07-143548-4 (alk. paper)
    1. Business ethics.   2. Disclosure of information.   3. Communication in organizations.   4. Social responsibility of business.   5. Corporate governance.   6. Transparency in government.   I. Title.

HF5387.038   2004
174'.4—dc22   2003025365

Dedicated to William Stanley Tannebaum.
May the light always shine from his eyes.

CONTENTS

ABOUT THE AUTHOR

Richard W. Oliver, Ph.D. is the CEO of American Learning Solutions. He is the author of a number of influential books, including *The Shape of Things to Come* and *The Coming Biotech Age*.

ACKNOWLEDGMENTS

OPENING MY EYES TO TRANSPARENCY

When I first decided to write this book, I had a definite idea of what I thought transparency was all about. Unfortunately, my vision was clouded. Rather than a narrow treatise on the evils of pro forma and off balance sheet accounting in U.S. businesses, I found that transparency deeply touches virtually everyone on the planet.

In learning about transparency, I experienced a journey around the globe, peeking into places I had never heard of, and finding to my surprise that transparency truly begins at home. So let me be transparent: This book would have been impossible to write without the insight of a dedicated team of idea contributors, researchers, editors, and critics, including Susan Oliver, Tim Leffel, Mary Glenn, Jeannie Kahan, Sandler Passman, Martha Kallstrom, and Peter Miller. To each, a special thank you for opening my eyes to my many opaque misperceptions.

INTRODUCTION

The first order of business for any book on transparency is a clear declaration of what it's about.

TRANSPARENCY: ENOUGH SCANDALS TO GO AROUND

This book is not solely about the scandals in corporate America in the late 1990s . While corporate scandals prompted the book, it became readily apparent that transparency, or the lack of it, was a concern in virtually every aspect of life. Similarly, it is not about U.S. transparency issues. My research found that country after country was grappling with its own transparency issues.

At the same time that U.S. corporate scandals were playing themselves out, the world was watching the drama of UN weapons inspectors trying to find hidden weapons in Iraq; terrorists launching a secret attack on New York City and Washington; governments around the world racked by revelations of misdeeds and hidden agendas; and the very bastion of honesty and truth, the Catholic church, embroiled in scandal and systematic cover-up. And, not to be outdone, some of the self-proclaimed purveyors of integrity in the news were doing damage control over their own misdeeds.

Clearly, there is plenty of need for transparency; for every country and organization, and many individuals as well.

Transparency involves a wide selection of events, organizations, and issues of growing importance in every walk of life. The book argues that transparency is an essential ingredient of success today: in politics, business, professions, and in our social, cultural, and religious lives.

THE NEW TRANSPARENCY: SEEING IS BELIEVING

In ancient cultures, *hearing was believing*. In today's highly visible culture, however, we admonish: *Believe only half of what you hear, because seeing is believing!*

Transparency, it seems, has taken on a life of its own. It has moved over the last several hundred years from an intellectual ideal to center stage in a drama being played out across the globe in many forms and functions.

An older, passive view of transparency has given way to a *new* transparency; transformed from a mere intellectual curiosity to a real-life, real-time requirement that engenders a range of emotional responses. It has gone from a reactive opportunity to a proactive requirement. It blossomed from a simple ideal to a complex set of expectations and regulations. It has touched off an international debate on morals, ethics, privacy, politics, and personal responsibility.

Transparency has also spawned a growing horde of government and nongovernment organizations, launched a legion of transparency professionals, and created an entire industry of transparency hiders and seekers.

The new transparency implies several important characteristics that are profoundly different:

- An *inevitable* trend toward more transparency rather than less
- More *intense* scrutiny from more groups and individuals around the world
- More *comprehensive* demands for new kinds of information
- More *lasting consequences* of action or inaction
- More *complex* requirements in gathering, analyzing, and reporting information
- More *proactive attention* by both the observer and the observed
- More *contentious* debates about what information should be public

TRANSPARENCY: THE RIGHT TO PRIVACY VERSUS THE PUBLIC'S RIGHT TO KNOW

As illustrated in Figure I.1, throughout history, major public issues have been about property rights: the right to own private property; the right to use (or abuse) public property; the conflicting rights to information property; and, in the near future, the rights of genetic property.

Today we are in the middle of a global public wrestling match on the issue of *information property rights*. Transparency, the debate du jour, is simply the flash point at the intersection of the *public's right to know* and the individual's or organization's *right to privacy*.

This book does not try to settle that argument; no one book could. It does, however, sketch out in broad terms the inevitable march of the forces propelling the world to greater and greater levels of transparency.

This propulsion toward more transparency comes from two sources:

- Increasing interdependence between countries and cultures
- Insatiable information technologies that daily supply and demand more transparency

Shakespeare wrote of Julius Cesar:

He is a great observer and he looks
Quite through the deeds of men

—Act 1, Scene 2

Such sentiment seems to pervade much of what is referred to throughout this book as stakeholders: those who believe they have a *stake* in an organization or the actions of an individual. They are playing an increasingly important role in the transparency drama.

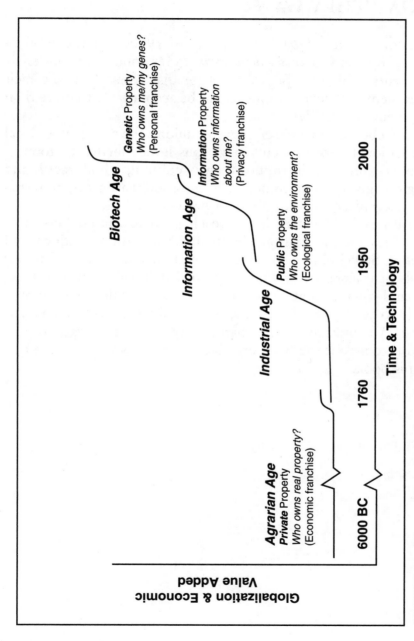

FIGURE I.1   Historical Life Cycle of Property Rights.

STAKEHOLDERS: WHO THEY ARE, WHAT THEY WANT

The concept of *stakeholders* began in the 1960s with the publication of Rachel Carson's *Silent Spring*. Her concerns about environmental pollution began a debate that resulted in the tacit agreement that corporations had to be accountable to more than just their shareholders.

Stakeholders include employees; unions; the public (both local and national); governments at various levels; media; customers; suppliers; financial institutions; civic, cultural, ethnic/racial, and religious groups; citizen action groups; and various nongovernment organizations with broad or narrow agendas.

All stakeholders feel they have a legitimate claim to know vast quantities of information about an organization's actions and intents. Stakeholders are at the center of the demand for new levels of transparency. They have real political clout, and their demand for information will not go away. While no attempt is made to report on all of these groups, for the reader's convenience, Web links to the transparency-oriented organizations profiled throughout the book are listed in the Resources at the end of this book.

CHAPTER 1

TRANSPARENCY:

SETTING SIGHTS ON A MOVING TARGET

The truth is incontrovertible. Malice may attack it, ignorance may deride it, but in the end, there it is.

—WINSTON CHURCHILL

Transparency, or rather the lack of it, has risen to the top of the public agenda in almost every aspect of our lives. It's at the forefront in global and domestic politics, in religious and secular activities, in education, social and cultural affairs, in matters as critical as a UN debate and as incidental as an ingredient list on a food label. But perhaps the most dramatic is its influence in business and economics.

One has only to turn on the television or radio news or read a newspaper to hear the questions "Who knew what when?" "Why was it not disclosed?" "Was there an intent to deceive?"

These and many similar questions, sharp and unequivocal, go to the heart of the matter. They demand answers about intent, hype, spin, dishonesty, cover-ups, manipulation, deception, fraud, ruses, trickery, scams, duplicity, cheating, lying, deceit, cons, corruption, and treachery. It seems there is an endless supply of negative words and deeds that lurks just outside the reach of this simple idea of transparency.

With transparency, you don't need all those other words. Without it, you have enough words to fill a dictionary.

From Watergate to the Middle East to Martha Stewart, it seems that the cover-up, or rather *the lack of transparency*, now eclipses the event itself!

1

If transparency is so important, why has it become so hard to find? And perhaps more importantly, how will we know transparency when we see it?

In some sense, transparency is an oxymoron: How can we see something that by definition is invisible?

THE NEW TRANSPARENCY: A MOVING TARGET

The question "What is transparency?" can make for an interesting debate. It sounds like a simple question, but one that garners a wide variety of answers. Those answers are colored by content, context, point of reference, occupation, income, demographic group, emotional involvement, and a myriad of other factors. Virtually everybody's definition today is quite different than it was even 5 years ago.

In its simplest terms, transparency has three main elements: an observer, something available to be observed, and a means or method for the observation. Each of these three elements is changing substantially.

WHO'S WATCHING WHAT, WHEN, WHERE...AND WHY?

It is clear that the concept of transparency has undergone some fairly significant changes, over time, but particularly in the last century, when the concept or definition of what was or was not transparent changed dramatically. Likewise, and equally important, the medium, venue, or method for observation has changed radically as well. While the what, when, and where of transparency may be precisely defined (even if with some degree of angst), the why or motivator of the transparency act or event is problematic, often in the extreme.

Perhaps the most important change of all is in the implied *rights and responsibilities* of those watching and those being watched. Today, the whys of transparency are under constant and significant revision. It's relatively easy to define the observer, the objects under observation, and the medium through which the observations will take place. But the rights and responsibilities of both the observer and the observed are most often nebulous, uncertain, and subject to the vagaries of time and circumstance.

DEFINING THE NEW TRANSPARENCY

In a physical sense, transparency means that you can see through some medium to an object on the other side. It's a compound word created from two distinct concepts: *trans* meaning movement and *parent* meaning visible. According to the *Oxford English Dictionary*, the early English use of the word *transparent* meant, "having the property of transmitting light, so as to render bodies lying beyond completely visible."

The Latin preposition *trans* is used frequently with another concept word to create a new word that means "across, to or on the farther side," such as *trans*port (carriage), *trans*fer (to turn over to another), or *trans*lucent (partially visible). For our purposes, the important thing to keep in mind is the implication of *action*, *motion*, or *motivation*.

Most dictionaries today (perhaps just a little behind the curve of this rapidly evolving idea) describe transparency as "free from guile," "candid or open," or "forthright." The implication, for individuals or organizations, is that transparency is *allowing* others to see the truth, without trying to hide or shade the meaning, or altering the facts to put things in a better light.

In other words, transparency, as currently defined, is *letting the truth be available for others to see if they so choose*, or *perhaps think to look*, or *have the time, means, and skills to look*. This implies a passive posture or motivation on the part of the individual or organization under consideration. In today's broader public context, however, transparency is taking on a whole new meaning: *active disclosure*.

Several factors have led to this change: intense media scrutiny; the availability of cheap, ubiquitous information technology in the hands of virtually everyone; and the growing global belief in "the public's right to know." The old transparency (being open and forthright, should anyone happen to ask) has given way to a new transparency, more active in calling attention to deeds, both intentional and unintentional.

In other words, the idea of motion or action in transparency has returned to a much earlier understanding of the term, with motive shifting to the left of the equation—putting new *responsibilities* on the observed.

But, as we will see, the current debate over transparency is leaving the question of the *rights* of the observer less defined and open to increases in both the frequency and scope of demands.

TRANSPARENCY: SEEING IS BELIEVING IN EVERY ASPECT OF LIFE

Even though the discovery of U.S. corporate misconduct has grabbed most of the headlines in the past few years, transparency is not a new issue for corporate America. Neither is it just a U.S. concern or even a business concern, nor for that matter is it just a concern of organizations. It is high on the agenda of every organization and every individual.

As this book will show, transparency is now the daily bread of everyday life, an issue for both the average citizen and the high-flying Wall Street stock analyst. Today, being transparent is "table stakes" for politicians around the world or between a boss and an employee in a two-person company.

Transparency is the new watchword in every walk of life: economic, social, and cultural. Some might argue that transparency is a Western concept. But it is clear that individuals and organizations around the world, regardless of race, creed, or nationality, are embracing transparency.

GOVERNMENT TRANSPARENCY

Government transparency extends from the local town council to the federal government in each nation. It is also an issue for global governments and quasi-government bodies such as the United Nations, the World Trade Organization (WTO), the International Monetary Fund (IMF), and the World Bank. There are also a number of large and powerful regional bodies whose reputation is affected by transparency, including the North Atlantic Treaty Organization (NATO), North American Free Trade Agreement (NAFTA), the European Union, and dozens of trade groups.

There is never a shortage of crises around the world, and there probably never will be. Dictators, rogue regimes, and civil wars seem to be an almost inevitable part of our history. However, as communication has increased throughout the world and international news has expanded via satellite TV and the Internet, the push for transparency is often quicker and more widespread. Much of the increased prosperity in countries such as South Korea, Thailand, Chile, and the Czech Republic has come from an open, democratic system where the governments' actions can be clearly scrutinized.

Transparency International (a global organization dedicated to curbing corruption in international transactions) defines transparency as "a principle that allows those affected by administrative decisions, business transactions or charitable work to know not only the basic facts and figures but also the mechanisms and processes. It is the duty of civil servants, managers and trustees to act visibly, predictably and understandably."

Organizations such as the IMF often tie aid and loans to levels of transparency (even though they occasionally come under fire for not being open enough themselves!). IMF guidelines for government transparency focus on four key aspects:

- Clarity of roles and responsibilities
- Public availability of information
- Open budget preparation, execution, and reporting
- Assurances of integrity

The large, bureaucratic organizations such as the UN and IMF are the ones most often criticized for a lack of transparency. Although they don't receive donations directly from citizens, they depend on funding from governments to survive. When a perceived lack of transparency exists, skirmishes over funding and reporting often result, as the rift between the United States and the United Nations over the past several years illustrates. One of the many issues surfacing in the antiglobalization protests taking place throughout the world is the secrecy behind decisions by the IMF and the World Bank. In order for these organizations to have credibility and respect, their actions must be as transparent as the actions they demand of donor recipients.

COMMERCIAL TRANSPARENCY

Most media articles about transparency concern business, more specifically the conduct of publicly traded companies: their accounting methods, earnings, insider trading, conflicts of interest, executive compensation, and the independence of their board of directors. In the simplest terms, *all stakeholders* in the organization want to know all the facts about a company's financial health and structure, including whether each officer and board member is acting in the interest of the shareholders, employees, customers, and the public.

Transparency extends to every facet of business and can both affect, and be affected by, the conduct of employees at all levels. For most businesses, success results from the ideas and actions of employees. A transparent organization will attract the best and retain the best. An opaque organization will continually deal with high turnover or a disgruntled workforce. Transparency also has an impact outside the organization—on customers, suppliers, global trade, and adherence to government regulations.

Over the past 50 years, world trade has increased exponentially. Without clear contracts, open pricing information, and defined tariff structures, none of this would be possible. Transparency allows all players to compete on a level playing field. Transparent trade policies increased the standard of living in developed nations and in Eastern Europe, Asia, and Latin America. Transparency also created pressure to improve conditions in third-world factories and to improve environmental and labor practices.

TRANSPARENCY IN THE PROFESSIONS

Those who hold an allegiance to a function, such as accountants, athletes, actors, lawyers, journalists, teachers, and doctors, are deemed professionals. By the very word *professional*, we assume that whatever service or function performed is transparent as to motivation and action. In fact, many have taken an oath to serve in the public interest. Therefore, when lack of transparency is discovered, the act seems even more grievous. Even more important perhaps is the skill, or, in some cases, lack of skill with which they render their service or function. Not surprisingly then, more and more of the public professions, such as doctors or lawyers, are finding themselves graded, with the results available in the press and on the Internet.

TRANSPARENCY IN NONPROFIT ORGANIZATIONS

Many charity organizations control a budget larger than the gross national product of small countries and wield tremendous influence in the regions where they operate. Their actions can literally mean the difference between life and death. Nonprofit organizations are ranked (by the media, for instance) on how efficient they are with donor dollars (how much goes to aid, how much to overhead), as well as their record of accomplishments. If their records are opaque and they cannot account for donations, they face a crisis in both their budget and their relationship with local leaders. Transparency is also critical to the credibility of international bodies, from relatively small nongovernmental organizations (NGOs) like Greenpeace to huge global NGOs like the Red Cross.

An organization that depends on contributions from donors is under the microscope like no other. People vote with their wallet in the commercial decisions they make every day, but they are even more likely to vote with their wallet when it comes to charity. This kind of expenditure is frequently the most emotional, so the decision often comes down to comfort and confidence. If a nonprofit organization appears to be hiding something or has lost face through a public scandal, donations are certain to plummet and may take years to recover.

TRANSPARENCY IN RELIGIOUS INSTITUTIONS

Religious institutions often struggle the most when it comes to transparency, using the defense that their actions are between them and God. As with any organization that is serving a defined set of stakeholders, however, a lack of transparency can quickly cut off the spigot of donations and leave the institution without the unwavering support of its parishioners. In order for organized religion to function and thrive, it must be able to clearly account for its financial and spiritual balance sheets.

Beyond the financial issues lies the much deeper and more important issue of spiritual trust. A lack of transparency can seriously weaken the trust and belief that followers have in organized religion and the clergy. For many, it is almost axiomatic that the secular world lacks transparency. But transparency and trust are the very foundation of organized religion. Therefore, revelations about the lack of transparency by clergy and religious denominations raise significant issues for the individual believer.

TRANSPARENCY IN INVESTMENTS

The twentieth century was marked by the gradual accumulation of government-paid benefits to individuals. The twenty-first century may well be characterized by the gradual reduction or elimination of many of those programs. The result is increased reliance on individual investments. Americans responded to these changes and aggressively poured billions of dollars into various Individual Retirement Accounts (IRAs) and other investments.

About half of American families now own stock, either directly or through mutual funds. For the market to function, the system must be transparent. As capital markets moved from acceptable levels of transparency for professional investors managing huge portfolios, to the average citizen investing his or her retirement money, the public focus shifted sharply to demand a whole new level of transparency.

OPACITY: WHO SUFFERS?

It doesn't take any imagination to see the widespread damage that occurs when opacity, or lack of transparency, is encountered. The last few decades of U.S. history provide plenty of examples. The dollar amounts and emotional destruction that occurred in the following (just to name a few) are staggering.

- The Watergate cover-up that led to the downfall of a President and his administration
- The savings and loan scandals that required a massive U.S. government bailout
- The tobacco industry's failed disclosure about the harmful effects of nicotine
- Revelations that the International Olympic Committee's members participated in outright bribes and questionable under-the-table deals in choosing host cities
- Massive accounting scandals at Enron, WorldCom, Xerox, and others that lost billions for investors and put tens of thousands of people out of work
- Cover-ups within the Catholic church that allowed known pedophiles to work with children

In all of these cases, a wide range of stakeholders suffered, whether investors, employees, banks, customers, or parishioners. A lack of transparency by a few led to a long list of losses for many, and an erosion of trust for everyone.

TRANSPARENCY: NOW YOU SEE IT, NOW YOU DON'T!

There's no magic formula that makes some organizations thrive while others fade away, and there are shelves of advice books illustrating different paths to success. History proves, however, that those organizations and individuals that continually hide the truth merely postpone the inevitable. Transparency may not lead to immediate success, but a lack of transparency can surely lead to swift failure.

In a capitalist market system or a democratic government, transparency is not a luxury, a sometime thing. It is now a fundamental requirement of the system, whether it's the economic, political, or religious system. In order for a market, local or global government, the church, or any other organization to work properly, the essential facts must be open and freely available to every stakeholder or citizen.

The balance of this book provides the reader with a comprehensive overview about important aspects of transparency: mistakes to avoid, strategies to deal with it, and programs to implement it.

CHAPTER 2

THE OPACITY SPIRAL:

DEFIANCE, DISCLOSURE, AND DESTRUCTION

Three things cannot long be hidden: the sun, the moon, and the truth.
—CONFUCIUS

During the late 1990s almost every organization in the world was nearly paralyzed with fear of what had become known as Y2K. The concern was that computers were not programmed to handle the date change at the turn of the century. The prognosis was that the world, particularly commerce, would be totally disabled at the first second of the new century.

Who could have known that it wouldn't be modern computers, invented in America in the late twentieth century and running virtually every aspect of our lives, but backroom accounting systems, invented by the Italians in the 1300s, that would turn business on its head as the clocks rolled over to announce a new millennium?

As it turned out, computers handled the change rather admirably. The accountants did not.

What had really changed was not the date but a worldwide attitude favoring near total transparency. It wasn't a clock tick that announced the new era, but a series of violent eruptions in financial markets created by system failures in the ethical standards of some very high-profile businesses. While everyone was watching the clock, the world transformed itself. Like it or not, transparency is here to stay.

SO, WHO REALLY WANTS TO BE TRANSPARENT?

"But I don't want to be more transparent!" You can almost hear some individuals and organizations saying that as you study their actions and read between the lines in their interviews. "Knowledge is power," some think, "and I'm not giving any away!" Some will fight the trend, often to the point of destruction. Others seek compromise. Some small public corporations are privatizing to avoid the costs of compliance, while still others proclaim that transparency threatens disclosure of competitive intelligence.

The lessons of history are unmistakable: transparency is no longer a sometime thing. It's here to stay. And like the sailors in Edgar Allen Poe's maelstrom (those caught in the vortex of opacity), the ride can be deadly. Transparency is even creating its own truths.

THE TEN TRUTHS OF TRANSPARENCY

1. What's done in private is eventually public.

2. What's acceptable today probably won't be tomorrow.

3. If it looks bad today, tomorrow it'll look worse.

4. Today's penalties will be worse tomorrow.

5. Each denial generates more pressure to disclose.

6. With each denial, enemies and detractors multiply.

7. With each denial, more friends desert you.

8. The more denials, the more severe the punishment.

9. Covering up is more damaging than the original act.

10. Nothing is forgotten, and seldom forgiven.

INEVITABLE END: THE OPACITY SPIRAL

Opacity, the opposite of transparency, is defined as the state of being hard to understand, not clear or lucid. When information is not clear, it's not trusted. When information is hidden, it's natural to believe there's truly something to hide.

Over and over, individuals and organizations get trapped in opacity's predictable pattern. See Figure 2.1. A person or organization commits an act in secret. Word leaks out. Denials follow. More information leaks out. Denials continue. Irrefutable evidence comes out. Eventually, the organization or individual is damaged or destroyed by the unrelenting spiral of media exposure, public pressure, and many times, litigation.

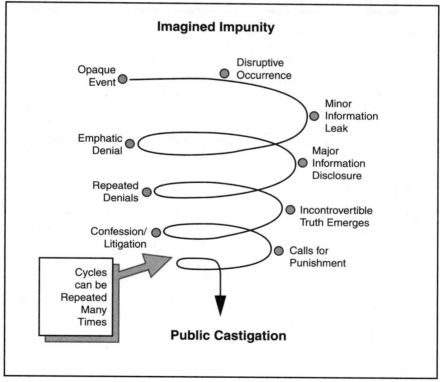

FIGURE 2.1   The Opacity Spiral.

Most transparency scandals, both historic and recent, follow this pattern. The spiral applies to politics (Watergate, Iran-Contra affair, Clinton sex scandal), financial markets (S&L crisis, BCCI, Enron, WorldCom), nonprofits (the Catholic church, Feed the Children, United Way) and many other cover-ups involving the misuse of funds or résumé inflation.

The Baptist Foundation of America (BFA) filed for bankruptcy in 1999, with its mostly elderly investors losing more than $590 million in the process. It was hailed as the largest bankruptcy of a religious nonprofit in the history of the United States. Arthur Andersen was their outside auditor. In a sign of things to come, Andersen was accused of ignoring fraudulent off-balance

---

ARTHUR ANDERSEN ENTERS THE VORTEX

Arthur Andersen's history as an accounting firm began in 1913. The firm was highly regarded as an honest broker when the United States struggled with the effects of the 1929 stock market crash and the depression. The company founder (for whom the firm is named) insisted that honest accounting and the elimination of conflicts of interest were essential keys to restoring the general public's faith in business. He argued repeatedly that public accountants were answerable to investors, not the companies they audited. If a client wasn't honest, the audit contract wasn't worth having. And that was how it operated for nearly a century.

Opaque Events

Andersen was involved in numerous opaque events over the years, but managed to stay alive through it all, partly due to a lack of media attention and public pressure. Clients WorldCom and Enron, however, were their undoing.

Disruptive Occurrence and a Small Information Leak

Andersen was jolted by a disruptive occurrence: numerous public accusations of fraudulent accounting and rumblings from financial analysts, accusing Enron of being a financial house of cards.

Denial

Andersen immediately claimed that the firm's audits were correct.

More Information Leaks Out

The SEC launched a formal investigation of Enron's finances in October 2001. The company was forced to restate 5 years of financial statements to account for nearly $600 million in losses. A month later Enron filed for bankruptcy, and Andersen's clients began to leave in droves.

Repeated Denial

Andersen continued to insist that the firm was not responsible for any wrongdoing. Andersen appeared before Congress and defended its work.

Irrefutable Truth Emerges

In January 2002, however, the Department of Justice launched a criminal investigation into Andersen, and the company admitted that its staff shredded thousands of documents related to the case.

Confession and Litigation

Just 3 months later, Andersen was charged with obstruction of justice. Amid the rapid exodus of clients, staff in overseas offices, and partners, the Chief Executive Officer (CEO) resigned. By April, the company announced that it would cut 25 percent of its U.S. workforce.

Calls for Punishment

Public pressure on the U.S. government increased, however, especially from Enron investors, as information of wrongdoing at Andersen and Enron continued to emerge.

Public Punishment

On June 15, 2002, the firm was found guilty of obstruction of justice. Its reputation had been shredded as badly as the documents it destroyed. Andersen was ordered to cease auditing public companies by the end of the summer.

Epitaph for an Honest Auditor

At the beginning of the Opacity Spiral, Arthur Andersen had 85,000 employees worldwide, with over 2000 clients and $9.3 billion in annual revenues. The end of the spiral was spent selling off assets and closing its doors forever.

sheet shell companies, ignoring the claims of knowledgeable whistleblowers, altering documents, and ignoring other rather obvious red flags.

Throughout the go-go bull market that reigned throughout the late 1990s, Andersen, like many others, began to let the line between consulting and auditing blur. They realized that the opportunity to win lucrative consulting contracts depended on no-hassle audits. Accusations of wrongdoing surfaced in Andersen's work with Sunbeam, Waste Management, and Asia Pulp and Paper. Andersen settled lawsuits related to Sunbeam for $110 million and was fined $7 million by the Securities and Exchange Commission (SEC) in the Waste Management case.

It was their entry into the Opacity Spiral.

A spiral of events that can bring down a company like Arthur Andersen can, in theory, be set off by a single event. When the truth comes out, however, this is seldom the case. Often a pattern emerges. Andersen's problems with Enron were not isolated. In addition to the cases mentioned previously, Andersen was also the accounting firm overseeing WorldCom. There, Andersen *failed to notice* a $3.85 billion shifting of funds to cover up revenue shortages. Further fraud totaling close to $4 billion was discovered in past years' reports.

WorldCom, for its part, demonstrated a pattern of hiding or misreporting information. An internally commissioned report released in 2003 described the company as "the poster child for corporate governance failures." Its board of directors "rarely scratched below the surface" as their main role became enriching the company's CEO with outlandish compensation. Their downfall was inevitable.

And, it's all so predictable!

HERE WE GO AGAIN: PATTERNS IN THE OPACITY SPIRAL

The Opacity Spiral occurs with such predictability that it's relatively easy to reach a number of conclusions about its actions and effects.

Once the spiral starts, it is difficult to stop.

Once an organization enters the spiral, the disruptive occurrence is usually just the tip of the iceberg. Mounting information leaks regarding pedophile priests in Boston eventually led to evidence of a widespread cover-up in the Catholic church. A whistleblower's accusations at one tobacco company led to evidence that the whole industry had conspired to squelch findings of nicotine addiction. For both, the legal and public perception cost was enormous. Politicians and TV ministers were brought down by sex scandals they first tried to deny. Charities saw an exodus of donors after mounting evidence of misappropriation emerged.

Truth has a habit of emerging just when it can do the most damage.

The wider the spiral (the gulf between truth and confession), the worse the outcome.

One reason there was such a swift "off with their heads" reaction to recent financial scandals was the repeated refusal to take responsibility. Denial after denial increased the public wrath, especially with investors and employees who lost their savings along the way. With each denial, in the face of mounting evidence of wrongdoing, the public cries for mandatory jail time increased. For WorldCom, Enron, and Andersen, the punishment of the companies themselves was swift and merciless. Many individuals associated with those companies are now facing civil and criminal litigation with severe penalties.

The longer the spiral (in time and events), the harsher the public punishment will be.

A drawn-out spectacle of denial and litigation can be fatal. Every week brings more bad news. The organization becomes a pariah. Business partners choose safer alliances. Politicians follow the public sentiment. Customers start viewing the organization negatively and decide to do business with a competitor instead. After months or quarters of this activity, winning a legal case can be a hollow victory.

Waste Management, for instance, has spent the years since its 1998 scandal broke settling lawsuits and struggling to survive. In 2003, 5 years later, its credit rating finally poked above the junk status level. According to the United Way, the funds diversion scandal that occurred there over a decade ago still comes up in surveys as a reason people won't donate to the charity organization. WorldCom emerged from bankruptcy as MCI: The old name is too tainted to ever use again, but the company seems to face daily challenges in the transparency of its operation.

THE END OF OPACITY

As the Opacity Spiral graphically demonstrates, no important event, big or small, personal or private, can forever avoid being sucked into its gravitational pull. Opacity is inevitably eliminated by the vicious cycle of public exposure. Transparency has become its own self-fulfilling prophecy.

CHAPTER 3

THE TRANSPARENCY IMPERATIVE

Electrical information devices for universal, tyrannical womb-to-tomb surveillance are causing a very serious dilemma between our claim to privacy and the community's need to know. The older, traditional ideas of private, isolated thoughts and actions—the patterns of mechanistic technologies—are very seriously threatened by new methods of instantaneous electric information retrieval, by the electrically computerized dossier bank—the one big gossip column that is unforgiving, unforgetful and from which there is no redemption, no erasure of early "mistakes."
—THE MEDIA IS THE MESSAGE, MARSHALL MCLUHAN AND QUENTIN FIORE, 1967

It's the postwar boom of the late 1950s. Mr. Ken Smith and his son Ken, Jr., walk into the local car dealership to purchase a new automobile for Ken, Jr., who is going away to college. The dealer *has all the information* needed to figure out how much money he is going to make on the transaction.

The Smiths have little information. The transaction is opaque.
The Smiths don't know the dealer cost of the new car, the trade-in value of their current vehicle, the option values, or even how the new car compares to its competitors in features or reliability. They don't even know what kind of gas mileage to expect. The father wants to show his son who's boss, however, so he negotiates with the dealer and manages to knock the price down 5 percent below asking price. Ken, Jr., later tells Mom that Dad really drove a hard bargain.

Fast-forward a half-century to the early 2000s.

Ken, Jr., and his son, Ken III, have been eyeing several different sports cars for Ken III as he prepares to go off to college. First they spend a couple of hours doing research on the Internet. They know precisely how the cars compare, which ones are likely to depreciate the least, which ones will require the fewest repairs, and how the options are priced in relation to similar vehicles.

The Smiths know virtually everything they need to know. The transaction is transparent.

The Smiths know how much the dealer paid for the car, the cost of extras, what incentives are being offered to both dealer and customer, what the dealer and private financing rates are for that model, and what their current trade-in is worth. Then father and son go car shopping. When Ken and his son return with a new car, Mrs. Smith knows without asking that they paid a fair price. Ken, Jr., nonetheless, recounts for his wife his brilliant negotiation style.

Ken III, meanwhile, goes to his room and writes a short computer program to optimize the car's fuel performance and maintenance schedule. He then checks various Web sites to determine the results of the manufacturer's "racing performance model" of his new car. Ken III then manipulates the global car racing statistics to determine performance based on weather conditions similar to those in his new college town. Then Ken III calculates exactly how much his parents will need to give him to run the car...

COMMERCIAL TRANSPARENCY: THE DEMOCRACY OF DEMAND

The above story can be repeated for buying tickets for travel, a new home, a computer, investment products, or nearly any other major purchase. The name of the game has changed: It is commercial transparency for all consumers. Or as one observer put it: The democracy of demand has replaced the tyranny of supply.

This increase in transparency is also apparent in nearly any circumstance, large or small, local or global, secular or profane. The increased access to information applies to political voting records, surgery success by physician or hospital, a church's legal entanglements, an artist's previous sale prices, a book's actual sales, a singer's true radio play, insider stock sales, union actions, background checks on a new employee hire, or a used car's repair record.

There is a new Information-Transparency Cycle operating in every nook and cranny of the world, in forums important and trivial, repeated daily and moving at faster and faster speeds. It is a self-perpetuating machine that grows more important and pervasive by the moment.

INFORMATION-TRANSPARENCY CYCLE: VORACIOUS DEMAND

Information is the lifeblood of an increasingly transparent world. It has progressed from cave drawings depicting the movement of animal herds and the appropriate hunting techniques to the global information warehouse of information, resupplied continuously and instantaneously, with basically free, unlimited rights of consumption. From information available only to those lucky few nomads who stumbled into the right cave for the night, the world has moved to a vast information storehouse on virtually any subject, available inexpensively or free, at the time and place demanded.

The Information-Transparency Cycle (I-T Cycle) is self-regulating, self-funded, and answers to no superior power.

The I-T Cycle has become the most important, cybernetic (or closed loop, self-regulating) system in the history of the world. It is an insatiable system, capable of knowing all, telling all, and forgetting nothing. And rather than just dumping more and more information into a global mass of ineffable digits, technology is also "Google-ing" it into user-friendly, congenial, and amiable bites of knowledge that are easily digested by even the least sophisticated palate.

Thus, at the risk of mixing metaphors, technology has, simultaneously, created an entire new landscape *and* become the "seeing eye dog" for those who demand to know where we've been and where we're going, but are unable to navigate the massive landscape alone.

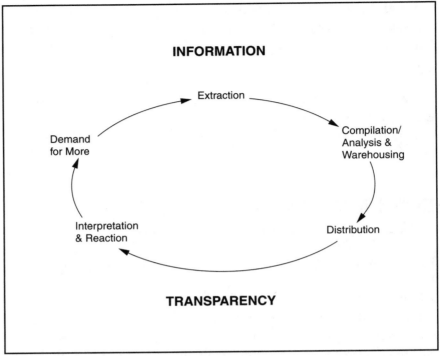

FIGURE 3.1   Information-Transparency Cycle.

The Information-Transparency Cycle is simultaneously an industry, an economy, and a way of life. It is both the fuel and the major mechanism of modern life. It operates independently and is answerable to no authority; but, most importantly, it is unstoppable. See Figure 3.1.

In the global I-T Cycle:

- Information is instantly collected on almost every subject or activity.

- Information is easily compiled, probed, analyzed, scrutinized, filtered, refined, prioritized, studied, stored, and manipulated.

- Information is directly and cheaply distributed to individuals or organizations globally.

- Reaction is immediate to what is there—or what is missing.

- More information is demanded, so more information is collected!

The global Information-Transparency Cycle is critically dependent on the ever-decreasing cost of information technology, or what authors McInerney and White, in *FutureWealth*, refer to as the "free fall in the cost of information." While such a free fall in information costs is daily more apparent in industry after industry, little attention has been paid until now to its impact on the state of transparency of people, places, things, ideas, ideologies, and actions. In every walk of life, whichever way you turn, technology has dramatically increased transparency. See Figure 3.2.

THE TRANSPARENCY IMPERATIVE

Today, information is a commodity; it is cheap and abundant, but rather than satisfying the world's voracious information appetite, it stimulates a hunger for more and more and more. In fact, the demand for information has become insatiable. The I-T Cycle, described above, feeds this voracious appetite.

The fuel that drives the I-T Cycle is an endless supply of near-free information. The machine that grinds it out is inexpensive,

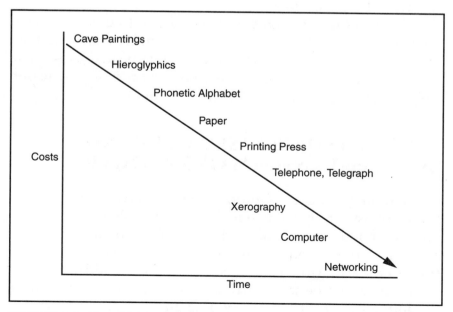

FIGURE 3.2   Free fall of information costs.

ubiquitous information technology in the form of telecommunications, computers, very tiny digital cameras and recording devices, personal digital assistants (PDAs), microscopic sensors, and hundreds of other digital devices for the collection, manipulation, storage, and transmission of information. The I-T Cycle moved very slowly over several millennia but has been ratcheting up to supersonic speeds in the last 50 years. Observing both the speed and global deployment of this new electronic technology, Marshall McLuhan described it as a global information *central nervous system*.

McLuhan's biological metaphor is prescient and apt. Like food and water, information has become something we can't seem to live without. Rather than being a rich, optional luxury, information has become one of life's vital necessities. Information stimulates the appetite for the relentless and unceasing demand for more and more transparency. It truly has become the globe's central nervous system.

The I-T Cycle, in the endless information gathering, manipulating, storing, disseminating, archiving, retrieving...and then starting over with more and deeper gathering...has created the new Transparency Imperative. The public's right to know is steadily and inexorably eroding the secret, opaque lives of individuals and organizations.

The Transparency Imperative unleashes a perverse mechanism: The more we know, the more we demand to know; the more we demand to know, the more there seems to be to disclose. The cycle seems endless. And the ever-decreasing cost of information technology suggests there is no end in sight.

FREE FALL: DECREASED COST AND INCREASED INFORMATION POWER

In 1965, Intel cofounder Gordon Moore observed that the number of transistors per integrated circuit was doubling roughly every 18 months and predicted that the trend would continue for decades to come. Moore's Law, as it came to be known, has held true ever since. Most observers expect this trend to continue until somewhere between 2010 and 2020. Figure 3.3 illustrates the author's projections to the year 2020.

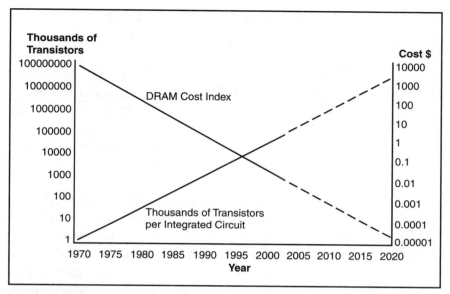

FIGURE 3.3   Moore's Law to 2020.

This doubling of computer power every 18 months has led to a host of other trends that affect both the capabilities and the cost of technology. In most areas, technology is so cheap that it has become a commodity. Consumers now get loaded PCs for under $500, a free cell phone when signing up for wireless service, and a 128-megabyte RAM card for $10. Phone calls are either a few pennies per minute or a flat rate for unlimited calls. The cost of commercial data storage drops every month.

This means that the cost of transparency—of retrieving, disseminating, and analyzing data—gets cheaper by the minute, with no end in sight.

For the first time in history, the information free fall creates all the necessary ingredients for a world of near perfect transparency: the right tools, at the right price, with the right incentives and drivers to make it all work seamlessly. The free fall in information also means that for the first time there is a power symmetry among the producers, disseminators, and demanders of information. No more scrolls secreted by the scribes; no more radio stations controlled by a few revolutionaries; no more hidden political, social, or cultural agendas—*equal access for all.*

LONG LIVE TRANSPARENCY: THE INFORMATION EMPEROR IS DEAD!

Once upon a time, there were the privileged few: the kings, their courts, and the scribes and clergy. These people had all the answers locked away, and their livelihood, or at least their individual positions in society, depended on it. In early wars, the victors would often first go to the temples of the conquered and destroy the sacred scrolls. These documents contained the secrets of the civilization.

Destroying them destroyed the enemy, not just physically but psychologically, not just temporarily but forever. By killing a few nobles and destroying a couple of key documents (such as chiseled stone tablets or papyrus scrolls), a small number of victors could control the large masses of the vanquished. The Romans ruled a vast territory because they created a new means of communication. As technology changed and the Romans didn't adapt, their empire collapsed.

In times of agrarian life and later in the era of mechanical, industrial technologies, controlling the limited means of communication meant controlling the masses. Whoever owned the means of communication controlled the political, economic, and social agenda. There was little incentive to be transparent and in fact, little demand to be so. Who knew to ask? But, perhaps more importantly, who had the means to ask?

With the advent of electronic technologies, first the telegraph and then the radio, a revolutionary's first action was to take over the radio station. From there, by controlling the means of communication to the masses, they could largely control the scope and direction of the revolution.

Fast-forward to today, and even the mightiest of politicians cannot control information flow. Even in the isolated dictatorships such as Libya or North Korea, leaders can "spin" but they can't control. Increasingly, every U.S. president from World War II on has decried the lack of control over information flow and, consequently, much of fiscal, monetary, and political policy. In politics, cheap information technology, from the printing press to radio and television, and now the computer and the Internet, has shifted power from the elite to the masses.

The fall of Communism in Eastern Europe is the direct result of new information technologies. These technologies lifted the Iron Curtain that carefully concealed the political and economic progress of the West from the view of the oppressed people in the East. It was information technologies, primarily interactive ones such as the telephone, the fax machine, and the Internet, that brought transparency to the masses of Eastern Europe for the first time. It allowed them to see, to organize, to revolt, and ultimately to bring down the Berlin Wall, the most visible political symbol of the lack of transparency in the twentieth century.

The Berlin Wall represented not just the restriction of physical movement, but the opacity of information about the rest of the world.

THE TRIUMPH OF TRANSPARENCY: CAVEAT EMPTOR IS DEAD!

This same transparency revolution occurred in commerce, albeit not as dramatically. Instead, it has crept up on us in small, seemingly insignificant, and often subtle ways. While escaping our conscious awareness, it has accumulated into a new reality that pervades every sector of our economy. Once, only real estate agents could tell you the selling prices for the houses in your neighborhood. Only your travel agent could find the best price on a flight. You phoned a dozen insurance agents or mortgage brokers to find the best deal on insurance or a house loan. Those days are now gone forever.

Commercial transparency means that buyers and sellers know all. The caveat emptor (let the buyer beware) mentality is dead. For the first time in history, every commercial transaction is, or at least, theoretically, can be, transparent. The new commercial reality is the triumph of transparency.

Very little that a business does is a secret anymore: not prices, hiring practices, customer service, or even gross or net margins. Technological progress has enabled anyone to find this information with a few mouse clicks. Government regulations, bowing to the pressure and pervasiveness of technology, let in the sunlight even more. With a public company, investors can immediately see every press release, every insider sale, and every form submitted to the Securities and Exchange Commission (SEC). Companies cannot provide information to mutual fund managers or stock analysts that they are not also providing to all other investors.

Moreover, customers can now tell the world about their good or bad experiences. Professional reviewers once held all the power and were often coddled by the providers. Consumer Web sites now allow praises and criticisms of everything from hotels to consumer electronics to credit cards. Products or services that may be ranked highly on technical merits can end up being criticized by the average user who has to live with them. It's an ongoing focus group, but one where the whole world is perched on the other side of the mirror.

TRANSPARENCY: POWER TO THE PEOPLE

Technology has empowered both decision makers and consumers with a wealth of information that would have been unheard of just a decade ago. Some of these developments had humble beginnings: The bar code allowed sales data to be recorded and distributed almost instantly, whether for books, CDs, clothing, or tubes of toothpaste. If a publisher is looking to sign an author or a music label is looking to sign a band, they can walk into a meeting knowing exactly what past sales figures are like.

For consumers, shopping around no longer needs to entail lots of driving time or phone calls; shoppers simply click and read. In the business-to-business world, sophisticated worldwide exchanges are in place for nearly every price-sensitive product, with prices and terms for the world to see. Many companies allow customers to check prices on a corporate Web site, even for complex software license configurations.

Charities are ranked on the percentage of donor money going for overhead. Parents know which school systems rank the

EBAY CHANGING SHOPPING FOREVER

While the Internet bubble grew, popped, and restarted with humbler goals, a few Web-based companies continued to grow rapidly. One of the most prominent, eBay, did so by creating a new and more transparent way of doing business.

eBay Creates a Worldwide Auction

eBay was conceived with a simple mission: to unite buyers and sellers of collectables on a standardized Internet trading platform. Other auction sites have come and gone, but eBay has continued to grow exponentially by encouraging pricing and customer experience transparency, insisting on clear rules of engagement.

Anyone who sells on eBay must register with the standard personal information, but the real key to the site's success is its feedback system. Every buyer and seller can receive feedback from the other party in each transaction. If the experience is good in each case, the person's feedback rating will be positive. If a buyer or seller is cheated, however, the resulting ranking and comments will be available for future transactions.

Browsers can easily compare the costs of similar items on the auction block including shipping costs. Bidding determines the true value of items, and potential buyers can see the final sales price of recently sold items. eBay is wildly popular because it's the most transparent marketplace in the world.

So is eBay a smashing success? With a market cap in the billions and profits exceeding half a billion a year, the company is doing very well indeed. From a free-market transparency standpoint, however, eBay is in a class all its own.

highest on standardized tests or college admissions. Potential clients can find out how well a law firm has done in court or which hospitals have the best track record in treating a specific condition. Nursing homes are ranked on how well residents have fared under their care.

In all these cases, as well as those involving reports on government leaders or institutions, the information is available for all to see and is archived for future reference. Transparency has put power in the hands of the stakeholders and consumers. It has changed the producer-consumer paradigm forever.

TRANSPARENCY'S BLIND SIDE

Cheap, ubiquitous information technology created the I-T Cycle, which begat the Transparency Imperative and then killed off the old caveat emptor. But, there is a downside. Some might call it a Blind Side.

While increasing transparency means that market mechanisms operate closer and closer to true efficiency, while consumers and stakeholders have more power, the privacy rights of both individuals and organizations slip slowly away. As Marshall McLuhan suggested in the quote that opens this chapter, the electronic technology monster never forgets and seldom forgives. Protecting legitimate privacy rights becomes a bigger issue by the second. While technology itself is amoral, its unrelenting onslaught may make striking a proper balance between privacy and transparency the challenge of the century.

CHAPTER 4

TRANSPARENCY:

TOP DOWN AND BOTTOM UP!

In evaluating people, you look for three qualities: integrity, intelligence and energy. But if you don't have the first, the other two will kill you.

—WARREN BUFFETT

Media stories on transparency often focus on what's wrong at the top: chief executive officers (CEOs) who report misleading, opaque, or even fraudulent financials; secret pacts between high-ranking military officers; or backroom deals among politicians.

While some leaders are culpable, creating a transparent organization is the responsibility of the entire organization. To be a truly transparent organization, four key elements are required:

1. A culture dedicated to openness and a commitment to transparency from an organization's most senior leadership

2. Programs and processes that encourage and ensure openness at every level, that reward transparency and mete out quick and decisive punishment for opacity, obfuscation, and fraud

3. Well-trained workers, managers, and administrators at all levels of the organization with the wisdom, integrity, confidence, and security to do and say what is right and to recognize and act when the organization or individuals are not doing things that should be done

4. Established means of proactive communication to the organization's important stakeholders

Obviously, this is a tall order for even the best organization, private or public, for profit or not-for-profit. But it can and must be done, if not voluntarily, then through public pressure, moral suasion, or legal and regulatory means.

LAYING DOWN THE LAW (AND MORE!)

The public's growing, and in some quarters, seemingly insatiable demand for information requires that boards and senior administrators embrace the *spirit* as well as the *law* of transparency. The Securities and Exchange Commission (SEC) argued as much itself: "The SEC strongly encourages companies to adopt codes [of business conduct] that are broader and more comprehensive than necessary to meet the new disclosure requirements." Even President George W. Bush called for this new standard. Understanding the law is decidedly easier, although far from perfect, however, than coping with the moving target of the spirit of the law.

But even within the law, uncertainty rules. Corporate reporting of financials frequently defaulted to volumes of information in an attempt, depending on the politics of the observer, to either comply or confuse. Regardless of intent, the result has been a growing mass of almost indecipherable data. In fact, just before he left office, SEC chief Harvey Pitt argued that the route to more and better corporate disclosure lay in simplified, shortened reporting that clarified and communicated public company accounts in a few pages.

Pitt identified the reverse of the Opacity Cycle. Every attempt by regulators to clarify information has had the opposite effect, touching off a high-stakes game of increased obfuscation. The history of regulatory reporting throughout the twentieth century is a "less than virtuous cycle" of accountants and lawyers finding loopholes or devising a creative path around virtually every new law, regulation, or accounting standard, often as quickly as they were put in place. But if corporate leaders embrace the spirit of transparency as a matter of principle and routine action, they'll give stakeholders the information they really want.

For business, the Sarbanes-Oxley Act of 2002 removed much of the choice and some of the confusion of corporate reporting (although it created much more confusion in some areas). New regulations eliminated many conflicts of interest: off-balance sheet financial trickery, personal loans for executives, and the slow reporting of insider stock trades. It also established jail time for those destroying evidence of wrongdoing.

Federal and individual state governments are using both civil and criminal courts to go after violators, most often those at the top, for example, board directors and senior management. Correct or not, the "buck stops there."

A CULTURE OF TRANSPARENCY

An organization's board of directors (or some other higher authority for nonprofits, and so forth) bears direct responsibility for creating a culture of transparency. Truly independent boards establish policies that ensure and reward transparency. They diligently monitor implementation, decisively intervene to ensure completeness, ensure that facts are not obscured and that conflicts of interest are eliminated.

Senior management's responsibility is to create the programs and processes to see that these policies are properly executed. In best practice organizations, top leaders are diligently committed to a culture of transparency. Not given to edicts from the top, or just mechanical processes of auditing, accountability permeates the organization and real commitments are made for collaboration and sharing information. Leaders create programs and processes that institutionalize transparency and make it an essential function and trait of the organization.

When top management has done its part, individual actions of employees make a transparent culture real. Those in the trenches are often most aware of how the organization is really functioning at the operational level, and as such, they bear equal responsibility for organizational transparency.

No organization in the world can claim victory when it comes to transparency. Like safety and quality programs, transparency is a journey, not a destination. Transparency requires constant refinements in response to new market requirements and increasing organizational competencies.

The following principles serve as general guidelines for organizational transparency:

- *Leadership commitment.* An organization's leaders are committed to the principles and spirit of transparency. They embed this commitment into the organization's communications with stakeholders, its information-gathering processes, and its systems of metrics. Commitment is demonstrated by the standards to which senior leadership holds itself, the documentation and communication of governance processes and metrics, and walking the talk with swift and steady enforcement of transparency and ethics guidelines.

- *Formalized processes.* Transparency requires frequent, abundant, and accurate information. Clear responsibilities for compiling and reporting of information metrics is assigned and automated where possible. Each relevant metric carries a reporting mechanism or process.

- *Training programs.* Top management's commitment to transparency is enhanced by comprehensive training programs that communicate this commitment and demonstrate avenues available to pursue it, including independent channels to report fraud. Managers are taught to collect, analyze, and report information that is decoded, that is, stripped of the jargon of the particular industry, organization, or profession, in an accurate but understandable way for nontechnical audiences. Employees are shown how to look beyond today's transparency requirements and attune themselves to the evolving demands of the marketplace. Training goes beyond the teaching documentation and reporting competencies, to the development of critical thinking and decision-making skills, and the encouragement of true understanding and commitment to transparency and ethical behavior.

- *Communication with stakeholders.* Today, transparency goes beyond just allowing interested stakeholders a look inside the company. Transparency demands *active disclosure*, including communicating essential information in a timely and convenient fashion and providing fast, easy, and inexpensive means of getting feedback. Transparent communication with stakeholders involves focusing on more than just the traditional numbers, such as financial data, customer statistics, and operational metrics. It requires venturing into accurate and understandable discussions of the stakeholder value drivers, the things that mean the difference between success and failure for the organization. Frequent communication to stakeholders is essential. Feedback from stakeholders (employees, customers, constituents, shareholders, community leaders) tells the organization what it is doing well and what it needs to work on.

TRANSPARENCY FROM THE BOTTOM UP: CUBICLE WITH A VIEW?

Transparency isn't limited to upper management, but is implemented in a systematic and pervasive manner throughout the organization. Those at the very top are often at the mercy of what goes on at lower levels. Some examples include:

- A marketing executive of a major soft drink maker rigged a series of test market results, overstating the popularity of a new product. Once uncovered, the fraud led to a multimillion-dollar payout and a damaged image.
- Several energy firms created a crisis in California and other states by intentionally gouging customers. One method used was to close some plants or keep capacity down at others in order to create artificial shortages. The wrongdoing was carried out in all levels of the organizations.
- Two major international drug companies were forced to cancel advertisements for high-profile drugs after the Food and Drug Administration (FDA) found that each company was blatantly misleading consumers.
- One of the country's oldest and most respected newspapers became embroiled in a scandal when it was revealed that one of its reporters routinely made up stories and claimed

to report from areas where he had never visited. A few top executives were replaced, but several lower- and mid-level editors had obviously turned a blind eye as well.

All major functions of an organization play a role in achieving transparency. A quick review of the standard chart of accounts [profit and loss (P&L), cash flow statement, and balance sheet] reminds us that transparency is needed at every line. What follows is a brief overview of how transparency is challenging the important areas of marketing, operations, human resources, and, of course, finance.

TRANSPARENCY AT THE TOP LINE: RECOGNIZING REVENUES

The first critical element for any organization is who is buying (or contributing or otherwise paying for) its products or services. What would seem to be rather simple, revenue recognition has in fact become one of the most perplexing aspects of transparent reporting. Huge volumes of accounting document how, when, where, why, and if a sale can be recorded. The sheer volume of minutia describing revenue reporting is beyond the ability of any one person to know precisely. As such, it creates huge opportunities, and perhaps incentives as well, to manage earnings.

Closely aligned with their responsibilities in accurate revenue reporting, marketing and sales functions play a critical role in organizational transparency, such as protecting customer privacy, making advertising claims that are accurate, creating truthful package labeling, and, most importantly, ensuring clear and honest communications and interactions with consumers and the public at large.

Transparency in marketing and sales is a function of the aggregated public view. Public eye refractions cannot be fixed by restating one line of a financial statement. Negative publicity from opaque sales and marketing techniques can backfire, often on a whole industry. While the music business spent millions fighting piracy, for example, some companies were defending

---

INNOCENT HYPE OR DOWNRIGHT FRAUD?

In the boom years of the 1990s one mutual funds company saw its coffers swell as the funds racked up huge gains on their mostly tech-related holdings. Flush with new advertising funds, the company increased its holdings even more by telling customers its analysts were out in the field working for them. Advertisements talked about analysts going into manholes to check on fiber optics jobs and visiting construction sites to see if a new shopping mall was being completed on time. In reality, the funds company actually had fewer analysts than its competitors, based on assets. Most of the analysts spent nearly all their time at their desk or at outings with the managers of companies in which they were investing. When the bubble popped and the stock market dropped like a rock, the company's mutual funds fell hard and fast as they were exposed for their deceptive practices.

Then there's the case of the software company sued in a class action lawsuit and forced to change its Internet marketing practices. The company was known for posting banner ads and pop-ups with text such as "You have 3 new messages" and "Click here to win a prize." Of course the claims were always completely false and were simply meant to direct unwitting consumers to the host's Web site.

---

themselves against lawsuits involving price-fixing, whereas artists sued others over improper accounting of royalties.

OPERATIONS TRANSPARENCY: GETTING IT RIGHT IN THE GUT

Transparency in an organization is not only about what's communicated externally, but about what's right on the inside, in the guts of its operations. Transparency best practice demands that the bowels of the company [the operation of its research and development (R&D) activities, product and service design, its manufacturing plants, shipping, delivery, retail stores, and after sale service] set the standard for the rest.

Transparency in operations, particularly in manufacturing, is focused primarily on compliance with countless regulations promulgated by such bodies as the Department of Commerce, Environmental Protection Agency (EPA), Occupational Safety and Health Administration (OSHA), and Food and Drug Administration (FDA). While some of this data is confidential, increasingly, regulatory results reach external stakeholders, either officially or leaked, particularly metrics on safety, health, or the environment.

Historically, although operations transparency problems haven't been news, they're becoming increasingly frequent, as the following illustrates.

- A pharmacy benefits management company was charged by federal prosecutors for canceling, losing, or destroying patient mail-order prescription orders on busy days in order to avoid penalties for delays. They were also accused of routinely shorting customers on the number of pills.

- Medical companies have continually popped up in the news for overcharging customers, routinely denying claims that should be paid, or submitting false records for government reimbursement. Often that fraud runs through several levels of the organization and has, in many cases, been institutionalized.

- Stakeholders are demanding more transparency on the question of how much of a company's workforce or outsourced work is being done outside the country. Which countries? And, what bodies or agencies are overseeing the environmental and working conditions in those countries?

HUMAN RESOURCES TRANSPARENCY: WHAT'S IN AN ORGANIZATION'S HEART AND MIND?

A public company's stock price today is often valued as much as four times higher on its intellectual property than on its plant and equipment. Intellectual property, by definition, comes not from the air, water, or ground, but solely from people. Thus, the success of every organization depends squarely on its human capital, the sum of its investment in people.

RÉSUMÉ INFLATION

Not all transparency issues emanate from organizations. Human resource departments and professional search firms deal daily with an individual transparency issue: résumé inflation. While job applicants are expected to put their experience in the best light, cases of downright fraud continue to pop up regularly. One survey estimates that one in seven job seekers lies on his or her résumé. Another study showed that fraud is most common with candidates earning $150,000 or more. In the first few years of the 2000s alone, snafus hit dozens of universities, where inflated résumé had been submitted by athletic coaches, professors, and even university presidents.

Outsiders, therefore, increasingly demand more information about an organization's *people policies*, including diversity, promotion, tuition reimbursement, union relations, personal use of the Internet, day care, AIDS in the workplace, health plans, retirement benefits, executive compensation, and succession plans, to name just a few. Many of these issues now merit annual reviews in the business press and public media. And, if that were not enough, on the near horizon, there are additional issues arising such as video surveillance, elimination of mandatory retirement, genetic testing, and biometric security.

The growth and nourishment of human capital, through the transparent development and execution of people policies, is largely the responsibility of an organization's human resources department. While traditionally responsible to simply set and evaluate people policies, human resource professionals are increasingly being called on to develop metrics and report, both internally and externally, on a host of human resource policies that heretofore have been private.

Likewise, they are increasingly being challenged to strike a very delicate balance between policies and procedures that facilitate transparency while protecting the privacy rights of individuals and the organization. While the human resources department designs these systems, it is up to the entire organization to ensure they work and to bring transparency problems to light.

To achieve internal transparency in human resource practices, many companies now use their Intranets to constantly update job postings, promotion lists, employee newsletters, position papers, and benefit frequently asked questions (FAQs). New regulations also require that all public companies provide safe, convenient, and secure whistle-blower hot lines for employees to report everything from fraud to sexual harassment.

FOLLOW THE MONEY: *TRANSPARENCY ON THE BOTTOM LINE*

No matter what an organization's purpose, function, or structure, the finance department's role is to accurately and completely portray its financial affairs. Financial reports include filings and documents required by law, as well as those expected by lenders, investors, employees, donors, or board members. Unfortunately, the insatiable demand for financial information, the speed at which it's required, and the increasing sophistication of financial tools, often sidetracked the finance department from its core responsibility: *clear and accurate reporting and analysis for shareholders.*

Nowhere, therefore, does transparency get more problematic than in financial reporting for public companies. Going back as far as the 1600s, financial reporting scandals have been the most visible and far-reaching examples of hidden information and outright fraud. In the twentieth century financial reporting scandals were a key component of financial collapses ranging from the Great Depression, to the Asian currency crisis, to the stock market meltdown at the turn of the millennium. Along the way, plenty of executives made the journey from business media star to inmate, and thousands of employees lost their jobs due to greed and fraud at the top.

The recent cases of opaque and fraudulent reporting are far too numerous to mention here. In the United States, new regulations have made CEOs and board members bear more responsibility, with signatures required on financial statements and a legal assumption that the CEO and chief financial officer (CFO) can attest to the accuracy of financial reports.

In many countries, however, the laws and even the voluntary requirements are far more lax than in the United States or Europe. When a global Generally Accepted Accounting Principles

(GAAP) framework is in place, however, as surely there will be, all companies around the world will meet the same transparency standards.

For nonprofits, nongovernmental organizations (NGOs), political think tanks, trade organizations, and the like, no such regulations are yet in place. Apart from limited tax reporting, full disclosure of finances and operations is strictly voluntary. But it is not a stretch to predict that change is in sight. Since 9/11, many social and religious organizations are under a new spotlight. And the calls for transparency in many other organizations are being heard. Every organization that depends on outside funding is, or soon will be, required to accurately and completely report much like public companies. And, frankly, there is every reason they should.

TRANSPARENCY'S NEXT FRONTIER: ORGANIZATIONAL VALUE DRIVERS

Much of the transparency debate today focuses on financial reporting. The next round of concerns is going to center on what is being called *organizational value drivers*. Financial disclosures primarily provide a guide to the past, a view out the rearview mirror. Value drivers attempt to look out the front windshield, and shine a light on where the organization is going and the factors that will take them there. Value drivers include areas such as intellectual property and talent metrics, organization competency analysis, and the like. Notwithstanding the difficulties of determining, collecting, analyzing, and normalizing such information (let alone concerns about competitive intelligence), demands for such information is already beginning in earnest.

TRANSPARENCY'S FINAL FRONTIER: INTEGRITY

As PriceWaterhouseCoopers notes in its report, *Transparency in Global Reporting*, "Rules, regulations, laws, concepts, structures, processes, best practices, and the most progressive use of technology cannot ensure transparency and accountability. This can only come about when individuals of integrity are trying to 'do the right thing,' not what is expedient or even necessarily what is permissible. What matters in the end are the actions of people, not simply their words."

In terms of transparency, that says it all!

CHAPTER 5

WATCHDOGS, WHISTLEBLOWERS, AND THE TRANSPARENCY POLICE

The truth is found when men are free to pursue it.

—FRANKLIN D. ROOSEVELT

Access to information is essential to transparency, but most people already have more data than they can deal with. So turning up the information crank would probably hurt more than help. What's needed is good analysis and context. When that's not readily available, a rapidly growing cadre of individuals and organizations known as *watchdogs* and *whistleblowers* are filling the void.

WATCHDOGS AND WHISTLEBLOWERS: PROFESSIONAL WORRIERS?

The term *watchdog* is a metaphor for a guard dog keeping an eye out for criminals, and has come to mean a group keeping an eye out for illegal or unethical behavior. Watchdog and advocacy groups often band together in an umbrella organization to deliver a consistent message with more clout. The Publish What You Pay (PWYP) organization, for instance, is supported by over 100 nongovernmental organizations (NGOs).

Its aim is to get natural resources companies to divulge what they're paying government officials for extraction rights.

The term "to blow the whistle on someone" dates back to the 1930s and is a reference to sporting officials or umpires calling a foul. The term *whistleblower* has come to mean someone who publicly denounces illegal, fraudulent, or wasteful practices, usually from inside an organization.

While at present there's no degree program for professional whistleblowers or a management association for watchdog organizations, they can't be far off. The number and scope of these kinds of organizations in the United States alone is staggering, and it's a fast-growing business around the world. Hundreds of thousands of people and organizations are now devoted to nothing but watching what's going on: in church, in school, in factories, in social club meetings, on farms, and in the halls of governments.

Some of these organizations, such as public accounting firms, have been in operation for a century or more. Others seem to spring up with the sunrise. With each new group, as with each new misdeed reported in the press, the voices for transparency grow louder by the day.

WATCHDOGS: WHAT'S GOOD FOR THE GOOSE...

While watchdogs are, in the main, professional, honest, and competent, some, curiously enough, have found themselves caught in their own transparency traps. Such ironies raise a fundamental question: "Who's watching the watchers?"

This chapter raises that question, while it profiles the growing body of professional transparency experts. Since the ultimate watchdog of almost every other individual and organization, of course, is government, let's start there.

FEDERAL GOVERNMENTS: THE FINAL AUTHORITY?

The world's biggest organization, the U.S. federal government, controls an umbrella of regulatory agencies that can be considered the best-funded group of watchdogs on the planet [although the Securities and Exchange Commission (SEC) argues it's stretched too thin].

After the stock market crash of 1929 and the onset of the Great Depression, the Securities and Exchange Commission was formed in 1934 to restore investor confidence. The law establishing the SEC required that public companies tell the truth about their finances and their inherent business risks and that those selling securities put investors' interests first. To accomplish its mission, "to protect investors and maintain the integrity of the securities markets," the agency oversees public companies, financial institutions, stock exchanges, and mutual funds.

Typical of the hundreds of other federal agencies that perform watchdog functions and ensure transparency are the Food and Drug Administration (FDA), which approves new drugs, oversees the safety of food production, regulates food and drug labeling and advertising; the Environmental Protection Agency (EPA), which ensures adherence to environmental regulations; the Federal Election Commission that sets and enforces policies on election campaigns and political candidate conduct; and the Federal Trade Commission (FTC) and the Departments of Labor, and Health and Human Services.

It's important to note that many such transparency functions are being "pushed up" to international bodies such as the United Nations Educational, Scientific, and Cultural Organization (UNESCO), World Trade Organization (WTO), and World Health Organization (WHO), or coordinate between countries as the issues become more global in scope. It's a sure bet that this trend will continue unabated.

STATE GOVERNMENTS: ASSERTING STATES RIGHTS

While many issues are handled at the federal level, states exercise significant power in some areas, including banking, business law, and transportation. This power has increased in recent years, as state attorneys general have filled a void left by federal inaction. States have won cases against investment banks,

---

WHO'S WATCHING THE WATCHERS?: PART I

Media are the main watchdogs over governments and function to expose wrong-doing. An Associated Press (AP) report, for example, brought to light a direct correlation between campaign donations and congressional voting records. Citizens action groups (listed in the Resources section) assist the media in this effort. Ironically, the media themselves, notably in the United States and United Kingdom, have been severely tarnished by transparency scandals of their own.

---

tobacco companies, drug firms, and music labels, in some cases winning agreements that observers say should have been legislated at the national level. Some recent examples:

- New York state levied huge fines and mandated that investment banks separate their research departments and investment banking divisions and create stricter conflict of interest disclosure guidelines.
- California forced all companies that have California customers to disclose any information-security breaches that have occurred in their company.

GROWTH BUSINESS: PROTECTING SHAREHOLDER RIGHTS

So many groups are advocating corporate disclosure and new governance standards to improve transparency that it has almost become an industry unto itself. They include pension funds,

---

WHO'S WATCHING THE WATCHERS?: PART II

CalPERS and other big pension funds and corporate governance centers at universities have been among the most active, clamoring for more corporate transparency. CalPERS shareholders, however, had to sue the fund to disclose some of their investments. Public pressure on venture capital funds for more transparency has led to some red faces at universities that had to disclose their investment losses for the first time.

WHO'S WATCHING THE WATCHERS?: PART III

In the past few years, longtime corporate governance rating groups, such as Institutional Shareholder Services (ISS), have been joined by a host of public and private organizations competing for the same role. These groups succeeded in getting policies that promote more transparency pushed through Congress or the SEC. While providing a valuable service, they have declined to make transparent how they do their ratings, or they charge a large fee to companies to learn more about their methods!

---

unions, governance rating groups, financial rating agencies, corporate associations, director groups, academic centers, think tanks, social investing groups, and organizations formed by individual shareholders.

Among the most important, pension funds wield tremendous clout in fighting for the interests of shareholders. California Public Employees' Retirement System (CalPERS), for example, controls over $100 billion for 2500 organizations, representing approximately 1.3 million government employees. Through its proxy votes and communications, the organization is a powerful advocate for shareholder rights.

Unions too are pushing harder for more disclosure. The American Federation of Labor–Congress of Industrial Organizations (AFL-CIO), for example, has been credited with pushing the SEC to adopt wider disclosure policies for mutual funds. These include more frequent disclosure of holdings and disclosure of how the funds vote their shares on corporate proxy issues.

The SEC often looks to stock exchanges to establish and enforce transparency guidelines. The New York Stock Exchange and NASDAQ have detailed policies on trading practices and company disclosure requirements, often going beyond what is required by law.

PROFESSIONAL WATCHDOGS: UNLEASHED

The line between shareholder advocacy and special interest advocacy is often a blurry one. Some organizations, such as the

Shareholder Action Network and CorpWatch, hold companies responsible for both financial and nonfinancial conduct. While this type of organization fights for clear financial reporting, they have won notable fights on uncontrolled executive compensation, as well as sustainability issues such as environmental policy and human rights practices.

Other pressure groups focus solely on one issue, such as the environment (Sierra Club, Natural Resources Defense Council, and Greenpeace), human rights (Amnesty International), and government corruption (Transparency International).

AUDITING FIRMS: FROM THE BIG EIGHT TO THE BIG ONE?

In theory, auditing firms were supposed to be the watchdogs for corporations, large nonprofits, and NGOs. At one time there were eight national audit firms. Economics drove them to merge until there were five. Transparency eliminated one more and severely shook up the others.

As the scandals of the past few years illustrate, auditing firms have not done a particularly good job of uncovering fraud or opaque reporting. Far too often, the Big Five accountant firms (now the Big Four after Arthur Andersen's collapse) allowed fudged numbers to stand or to keep problems hidden. In some cases, such as those involving off-balance sheet companies and tax-dodging strategies, it was the auditing firm itself that suggested to the client how to obscure information. Other bad business practices included using former employees as auditors, providing personal tax advice to executives, and tying auditing services to more lucrative consulting work.

It's no surprise then that the audit watchdogs attracted their own set of watchers. Audit watchdog groups, the media, and rating agencies continue to expose questionable practices. Weiss Ratings, for example, released a report in 2003 finding that auditing firms gave a clean bill of health to 94 percent of companies that were later deemed to have committed accounting errors.

After a spate of scandals brought these transgressions to light, sweeping changes followed. While there will always be

---

WHO'S WATCHING THE WATCHERS?: PART IV

In the past, the Financial Accounting Standards Board (FASB) was responsible for overseeing public accountants in the United States. After a series of financial scandals exposed major shortcomings in the system, public pressure for a more independent agency emerged.

As part of the Sarbanes-Oxley Act of 2002, the SEC formed a private-sector, non-profit corporation known as the Public Company Accounting Oversight Board (PCAOB). In its own words its mission is to "oversee the audits of public companies in order to protect the interests of investors and further the public interest in the preparation of informative, fair, and independent audit reports."

Unfortunately, its first proposed chair was deposed for potential conflicts that hadn't been disclosed.

Surprise! Yet another level of watchers emerges. Consumer advocate Ralph Nader launched the Association for Integrity in Accounting to monitor the new PCAOB.

---

room for improvement, the firms are now more actively delving into their role as an independent party that reports on the truth.

Some sections of the Sarbanes-Oxley Act relate specifically to accounting firms, with rules against some of the bad habits that were common in the past. Continued pressure from all fronts will likely keep the spotlight on accounting firms to ensure they are properly fulfilling their watchers' role.

IT'S OFFICIAL!: INSTITUTIONALIZED WHISTLEBLOWERS

Several whistleblowers took center stage in the financial scandals of the early 2000s, most notably at Enron. In many cases employees had formally complained about fraud and were either ignored or punished. In a high-profile, noncorporate case, a manager who was fired after exposing security problems at Los Alamos National Laboratory was awarded a settlement of $930,000.

Organizations now need to have processes in place to separate the valid claims from the false ones, with a channel for employees to make reports to an outside authority. In cases where fraud or other illegal activity exists, however, the increased legal protection comes with an implied responsibility. Every employee has the ability and the duty to bring fraud to light.

TRANSPARENCY POLICE: PULLING THE PLUG ON THE NET

As discussed more fully in Chapter 6, a free press is an essential element of transparency. A *Wired* magazine special feature recently highlighted the methods that governments use to keep the Internet's vast array of information away from its citizens:

- Some countries use a monitored firewall that attempts to scan, block, and blacklist traffic from offensive e-mail and Web sites. Vietnam blacklists 2000 sites.
- China reportedly employs 30,000 "e-police" to snoop on Net use and monitor chat room conversations. They keep a tight rein on Internet service providers (ISPs), who are required to block traffic on subjects ranging from Taiwan independence to outlawed social groups.
- Only 60,000 Cubans are able to send and receive e-mail, with about half able to receive international messages. The government requires prior permission to access the Internet from home, a privilege rarely granted.
- A number of countries use their telephone monopoly systems and high taxes to keep Web access out of the reach of all but the wealthiest.
- Citizens in some countries receive lengthy prison sentences for posting to or looking at sites that expose or criticize government policies.

CLEANING HOUSE

U.S. Supreme Court Justice Louis Brandeis is credited as saying, "A little sunlight is the best disinfectant." The ever-increasing number of watchdogs, whistleblowers, and watchdog-watchers should ensure that there are few places left to stash information away in the dark. And, as Chapter 6 illustrates, that's true around the world.

TRANSPARENCY:

GUIDING LIGHT FOR THE GLOBE

A lie can go around the world and back while the truth is lacing up its boots.
—ANONYMOUS

When international trade first began, there was no such thing as transparency. The Dutch East India Company and Britain's Hudson Bay Company were granted monopoly status by their governments and trade rules were fixed by force.

Thankfully, the world has come a long way. It's more transparent every day, not only in trade, but in many other ways as well.

GLOBAL TRANSPARENCY: WHO NEEDS IT?

The recent blackout in the northeast United States and parts of Canada did more than leave 60 million people in the dark. It was a graphic metaphor for how interdependent the world has become. The lights went out in a relatively small area of the two countries, but the blackout disrupted politics, commerce, and travel throughout the world.

Many organizations operating solely within their own country might think of global transparency as a lofty but irrelevant issue. At one time, they would have been right, but no longer. The world economy is now so interconnected that almost no individual, government, business, or any other organization is unaffected by globalization.

When a company anywhere is caught using fraudulent accounting methods, shock waves reverberate with customers, suppliers, and investors around the globe. When a government obscures farm subsidies or secretly violates trade agreements, it impacts global commodity and food prices.

Global economics and governance mean that transparency is now *the essential requirement* to participate in the world community.

FINANCIAL TRANSPARENCY: GLOBAL GAP?

A string of scandals on five continents at the turn of this century snared a host of global companies with extensive international operations. Despite these high-profile cases, most commerce is transparent. Multinationals operate under clear trading agreements and governments increasingly remove loopholes. China, for example, joined the World Trade Organization (WTO), binding the country and its companies to stricter international transparency standards.

GLOBAL GAAP

One obstacle to global financial transparency is widely differing national accounting methods. Traditions die hard, and local accounting principles are influenced by history, governments, and shareholders. The International Accounting Standards Board, based in the United Kingdom, and the U.S. Financial Accounting Standards Board are working to create standardized financial reporting methods for every nation. The goal: "Create a single set of high-quality, global accounting standards that require transparent and comparable information in general purpose financial statements."

If these global Generally Accepted Accounting Principles (GAAP) efforts succeed, investors and stock exchanges could confidently compare companies across the globe using identical standards. Current projections call for a standard set of reporting requirements adopted by 2005. Depending on local regulations, some nonprofit organizations will be required to follow suit.

One Asian study found that companies that emphasize corporate transparency experience a higher share price than their peers: "Transparency [means] identifying and reporting to investors the information needed to make decisions, not merely to satisfy minimum statutory reporting requirements. The market accords a premium…to the share price of such companies compared to its peers in the same industry and with similar financial performance."

TRANSPARENCY'S NEW REALITY: SUSTAINABILITY REPORTING

Transparency today, however, means going far beyond financial reporting.

The Global Reporting Initiative was established to set international guidelines for sustainability reporting, going beyond financials and covering the triple bottom line of economic, environmental, and social performance. The group notes that more than 3000 corporate, environmental, social, or sustainability reports have been published voluntarily in the past decade. Sustainability reporting helps, among other things, to "maintain and strengthen trust with community and advocacy groups, investors, consumers, and other stakeholders" and "reduce share price volatility and uncertainty occasioned by surprise, untimely or incomplete disclosure."

A GROWING GLOBAL MANDATE: WORLD LABOR STANDARDS

Globalization has led to an increased standard of living in many developing countries. While many companies brought western labor and work standards to the Third World, not all have been so enlightened. Moving production from high-wage countries to low-wage ones created severe criticism for some company's labor practices. Major reforms followed, and many companies are adopting a set of basic global standards and freedoms for workers.

TRANSPARENCY IN STYLE

The Fair Labor Association promotes adherence to international labor standards and better working conditions worldwide. The group advocates a Workplace Code of Conduct, based on the core labor standards of the International Labour Organization (ILO). It publishes annual reports on labor conditions in various countries, as well as conditions in individual factories. The organization is a unique coalition made up of nongovernmental organizations (NGOs), hundreds of colleges and universities that buy apparel, and a dozen consumer brands including Nike, Liz Claiborne, and Polo Ralph Lauren.

SOCIAL INVESTING: BEING REWARDED FOR DOING THINGS RIGHT

Comprehensive transparency exposes the degree of social concern inherent in corporate policies and practice. But corporations are economic, not social, creatures. So, are the two incompatible?

Socially responsible actions used to be their own reward, until transparency made it possible to do both good *and* well. Socially responsible investing has grown rapidly since the early 1990s, as some mutual funds attracted a great deal of capital and began wielding real financial clout. The first socially responsible global fund was created in 1992 and the Dow Jones Global Sustainability Index was launched in 2000. Some of the largest companies in the United States now offer such investments in their employee 401K plans. Big mutual fund companies, including Vanguard, also offer a socially responsible fund.

ENVIRONMENTAL TRANSPARENCY: LET THE SUNSHINE IN!

There is no shortage of global and local watchdogs for the environment. Pressure for transparency from large, well-funded global environmental groups, for example, helped international companies make huge strides in reducing environmental problems.

Today local community groups, environmentally focused political parties, media, and state and local governments are all playing a role in balancing environmental concerns with those needs of economic development. And now, it's all happening with plenty of sunshine.

GOVERNMENT TRANSPARENCY: CLEARING THE BACKROOM CIGAR SMOKE

A global corruption survey in 2002 conducted by Gallup and Transparency International revealed several key findings (see Figure 6.1):

- Corruption hurts the poor far more than the rich, with two in five low-income responders saying, "corruption has a very significant effect on their personal and family life."

- Six out of every seven people around the world think corruption has "a significant impact on the political life of their countries."

Several government financial crises in the 1990s threatened to destabilize world commerce, with the currency disaster in Asia being the most serious. The International Monetary Fund (IMF) admits to some responsibility, but the real culprit was a lack of clear and truthful information coming from governments. Leaders willfully obscured data on their international reserves and external debt until it was too late.

As the IMF explained subsequently, these crises led to a number of reforms. "A natural fallout from the sequence of crisis and response was that reforms that, in another epoch, would have proceeded quietly, without much public fanfare, now required active and constant public engagement." The IMF and World Bank dramatically stepped up their efforts in reporting metrics, stakeholder dialogue, and creating consistent measurement standards.

Ten least corrupt:

Rank	Country	CPI Score (on scale of 10)
1	Finland	9.7
2	Denmark	9.5
	New Zealand	9.4
4	Iceland	9.4
5	Singapore	9.3
	Sweden	9.3
7	Canada	9.0
	Luxembourg	9.0
	Netherlands	9.0
10	United Kingdom	8.7

(The United States appears at number 16, with a score of 7.7)

Ten most corrupt:

Rank	Country	CPI Score (on scale of 10)
93	Moldova	2.1
	Uganda	2.1
95	Azerbaijan	2.0
96	Indonesia	1.9
	Kenya	1.9
98	Angola	1.7
	Madagascar	1.7
	Paraguay	1.7
101	Nigeria	1.6
102	Bangladesh	1.2

FIGURE 6.1   Global Corruption Index. (*Source*: Transparency International's 2002 Global Corruption Perception Index. Note that the survey only includes 102 nations. Many countries with little data available, such as Cuba and North Korea, are not included.)

MEDIA TRANSPARENCY: NEW MEDIA MAKE TRANSPARENCY PERSONAL

One common thread runs through all of the above: access to a free press. In far too many countries virtually all news is produced by the government and dissenting opinions are quashed. According to Reporters sans Frontières (Reporters without Borders), countries with the least press freedom are (in order): North Korea, China, Burma, Turkmenistan, Bhutan, Cuba, Laos, Eritrea, Vietnam, and Libya.

It is no coincidence that many of these countries are also accused of having the most corrupt governments and committing the worst human rights violations. Without access to the Internet, impossible in North Korea and extremely difficult for ordinary people in most of the other countries, citizens have no access to information about the abuses.

In much of the world, however, satellite TV and the World Wide Web make many public press restrictions irrelevant. Those with access to the Internet or satellite TV can simply ignore the public media and use personal media for keeping informed. As access to the Internet grows, governments find it increasingly difficult to control the flow of information. If they keep out the Internet altogether (by restricting Internet service providers), they will hold back economic progress and their nation will fall further behind the developed world.

IT'S A SMALL WORLD AFTER ALL

Global trade and global government agencies have made the world a very small place, but the push for transparency is making it even smaller. If Marshall McLuhan were still around, he would probably declare that the Global Transparent Village was just slightly out of focus, but not by much.

CHAPTER 7

BEST PRACTICE:
REAPING TRANSPARENCY'S REWARDS

Success is the sum of small efforts, repeated day in and day out.
—ROBERT COLLIER

TRANSPARENCY SUPERSTAR: THE ORACLE OF OMAHA

No book about transparency is complete without reference to the superstar of investing, Warren E. Buffett, and how he has made honest earnings analysis, clear assessments of the future, and understandable explanations of executive compensation the hallmarks of his reports to shareholders. His company, Berkshire Hathaway, has amassed a huge fortune with plain old-fashioned logic, hard work, unwavering consistency to clearly stated investment principles, *and importantly*, to transparency.

Buffett tells it like it is and never minces words, even when it hits home personally. In a 2001 report to his shareholders, describing an investment that went sour, he said: "I've made three mistakes related to Dexter that have hurt you in a major way: (1) buying it in the first place; (2) paying for it with stock; (3) procrastinating when the need for changes in its operation were obvious. I would like to blame [the mistakes on]... anyone else ... but they were mine."

For over 38 years, Buffett has returned more than 22 percent compound annual growth to his shareholders, turning a $19 investment in one share of stock to one worth over $40,000 (per share book value).

Not content to keep his own house in order, he has sweet-talked, humored, encouraged, cajoled, insisted, and even demanded that the rest of the financial world join him in his pursuit of clear, honest, and comprehensive financial reporting.

An outspoken critic of such deceptions as pro-forma accounting, he used his 2002 annual report to make his point dramatically: "We've yet to see a pro-forma presentation disclosing that audited earnings were somewhat high. So, let's make history: Last year, on a pro-forma basis, Berkshire had *lower* earnings than those actually reported." Eschewing arcane accounting jargon, he goes on to explain how that happened in simple, crisp, and understandable English.

There is no more transparent reporting to be found than at http://www.berkshirehathaway.com/.

TRANSPARENCY: "I KNOW IT WHEN I DON'T SEE IT"

As Chapter 1 argued, transparency is an idea undergoing substantial change, its definition is in transition, and its targets are always moving. Unfortunately, the concept of transparency also lends itself easily to condemning the offenders and eulogizing those who went down with the ship.

It's difficult, therefore, to find good examples of those who believe in transparency and daily go about the business of doing the right thing. Ironically, its like the good guys are transparent! We tend to take notice, not of exemplary efforts but of major transgressions. In other words, with transparency: "I know it when I *don't* see it."

THE LONG WINDING ROAD TO TRANSPARENCY

As argued earlier, transparency is a journey not a destination. No country, no company, no organization, no individual is inherently transparent. It takes hard work and commitment to achieve it, and there are sure to be deviations along the way. That makes it easier to spot digressions than to cite organizations and individuals that are succeeding through good transparency practices. But the rewards are numerous for those who keep their compass pointed in the right direction.

Countries, such as in Western Europe, the United States, Canada, and Australia, with the strongest disclosure laws and practices tend to have the greatest long-term prosperity, both for their domestic companies and the overall population. While Japan remains one of the world's richest nations, it's been in a recession since the beginning of the 1990s, due in no small measure to the opaque financial dealings of its corporate sector.

A World Bank study found that transparency and increased standards of living require deliberate efforts. "First, the strategy of waiting for improvements in governance to come automatically as countries become richer is unlikely to be successful. Second, there is unlikely to be a 'virtuous circle' of better governance improving income, in turn leading to a further improvement in governance, and so on. Together, these two implications point to the fundamental importance of positive and sustained interventions to improve governance in countries where it is weak."

For business and other types of organizations, much the same can be said. Transparency doesn't just happen. It's a result of conscious commitment, long-term goals, carefully crafted policies, and consistent practice on a day-to-day basis.

What follows are four brief case studies where the long winding road to transparency paid big rewards.

FOUR SCORE WITH TRANSPARENCY

1. BRITISH PETROLEUM: GOOD GUYS DON'T FINISH LAST

Many big multinational companies wouldn't qualify as a poster child for transparency. But one, British Petroleum (BP), stands head and shoulders above the multitude. So how did BP, one of the largest and best-known energy companies, end up with such a stellar reputation?

With "actions speaking louder than words," BP has won over many of the industry's toughest skeptics, including environmental groups and social investing mutual funds.

BP routinely scores near the top in independent surveys. Business in the Community, a U.K. consortium of 700 companies devoted to improving their positive impact on society, recently released a Corporate Responsibility Index, with BP placing in the top quintile. The company also earned a 9.6 out of 10 from Standard & Poor's Governance Services, which measures corporate governance and transparency.

Putting Its Money Where It Can Be Seen

In a clear sign of its commitment to transparency, BP decided to reveal a $100 million signature bonus it paid to the government of Angola, a move that compromised future business dealings with the country. BP assumed its competitors would follow suit, but none did.

The company also dropped out of a lobbying group that was pressuring members of Congress to allow oil drilling in Alaska's Arctic National Wildlife Refuge. While it reserves the option to drill in the area if legislation passes with strong citizen support, it felt that backroom lobbying efforts were not in the interest of its stakeholders.

BP hosts a Web site that provides current information on its Caspian Sea pipeline project, with frequent updates on environmental impact studies, legal arrangements, and financial deals around the project. The site is available in English, Russian, and Turkish. The Web site (www.bp.com/environ_social) also details relationships with governments and other institutions and explains potentially murky situations in different parts of the world.

The company's annual report contains reporting on environmental and social issues and a separate report provides more details on water discharge, emissions, biodiversity, and impacts on local economies.

Inviting Others to the Party

The company has been a high-profile supporter of the Extractive Industries Transparency Initiative and also the Publish What You Pay initiative. Both are aimed at disclosing payments made by oil and mining companies to governments as a means of increasing transparency in the developing world.

The company also supports and participates in the World Bank Group's Extractive Industries Review, the World Business Council on Sustainable Development, and numerous country-specific transparency and reporting organizations.

A report from the Investor Responsibility Research Center cited BP and Shell as the only major energy companies to adequately report on greenhouse gas emissions and their efforts to reduce them. BP reported current results as a matter of course, but also took an innovative step ahead, projecting current trends into the future. Such prudent management of emissions creates a positive side effect: BP reportedly cut annual CO_2 emissions at their plants by 10 million tons, generating savings of some $650 million.

TRANSPARENCY'S BOTTOM LINE: THE PROOF IS IN THE PUDDING

So what's transparency's bottom line? Does all this pay off for shareholders?

In BP's case, the answer is a resounding "yes." The company's excellent financial track record is backed up by an Innovest Strategic Value Advisors study that closely examined how environmental risk can affect the shareowner value of oil and gas companies. Its conclusion about transparently managing risk:

- "Over the five-year period...the above-average companies, including BP,...outperformed the below-average companies... by approximately 17.3 percent."

- Above-average companies also outperformed the below-average companies in many other aspects, including operating profit per share (44 percent), price-to-book ratio (a 5-year average of 33 percent) and price-to-cash flow (a 5-year average of 49 percent).

With a steadily appreciating stock price and a high dividend, BP has shown that being a transparency leader in a tough industry can be good fuel for success.

2. CHILE: A TRANSPARENCY SUPERHERO EMERGES

As in many struggling regions of the world, economic and political transparency was not a watchword of Latin America during the last century. Tiny Chile, stretched a few hundred miles wide and 4000 miles long against the Pacific Ocean in the west, and geographically isolated by mountains in the east, had every excuse to be opaque, and stay that way. But it hasn't. The resolve and courage of its people was the light that shone through a sea of continental darkness.

Throughout the twentieth century, Chile suffered through many typical Latin American problems. The country survived political instability, food shortages, widespread unemployment, and a major earthquake. In the early 1970s, a disastrous political period was characterized by runaway inflation, violent protests, and finally a military coup. That period was followed by a brutal dictatorship that jailed opposition leaders, banned political parties, and stifled press freedom. This power gradually eroded until 1988, when the leadership stepped down. A new democratically elected government was installed in 1989, major reforms initiated, and the country began the rapid ascent that continues today.

From Last to First in Latin America

Transparency has been a key driver of Chile's success and has been a high priority of voters and elected officials. Government budgets are open to scrutiny and the press operates freely. There are powerful checks and balances within the government. The judiciary is independent and accountable, and the rule of law is highly respected in the business world.

Chile has also embraced technology and used it to increase openness. Government bids are conducted over the Internet. The central bank, which is independent, continually updates its finances and policies on its Web site, including frequent media interviews with the bank's president. Chile was one of the first countries in the world to privatize its social security program and allow its citizens to freely choose their own retirement investments.

The country has continually demonstrated a commitment to economic liberalization and open market policies. Foreign investors feel that they are competing on a level playing field.

As a result of this transparency, Chile has quickly become the economic star of Latin America. It now has the most stable, democratic, and transparent government in the region.

- Transparency International's 2002 Corruption Perceptions Index ranked Chile in 17th place, with a score of 7.5, similar to Germany (7.3), and the United States (7.7). Chile's position was by far the best in Latin America. Among emerging economies, Chile ranked third after Singapore and Hong Kong.

- One report ranked 35 of the world's major economies, based on five different measures of transparency for business: corruption, legal system, economic policy, accounting guidelines, and regulatory framework. In this report, Chile tied the United States as the second most transparent place, behind Singapore but ahead of the United Kingdom.

- Chile is rated the most competitive country in Latin America by the International Institute for Management Development (IMD) and the World Economic Forum.

- The country's credit score is ranked highest in Latin America by risk analysts Moody's, Standard & Poor's, and most top Wall Street investment banks.

Chile's economy has continued to grow throughout the global recession of the late 1990s and early 2000s and is expected by the IMF to continue growing steadily throughout the decade. Its openness led Chile to the front row of nations discussing free trade with the United States. With inflation and unemployment much lower than other South American nations, Chile has proved that transparency can have wide-reaching positive results.

TRANSPARENCY: COST OR COMPETITIVE ADVANTAGE?

The next two case studies show conclusively that transparency is not a "charge to earnings," but rather is emerging as a sure route to increasing competitive advantage, putting real dollars on the revenue line.

In Chapter 3, the story of three generations of the Smith family demonstrated how transparency has leveled the playing field when buying a new car. But as many people know, buying a used car is still an opaque transaction, at least until now. Carmax has applied the growing wealth of information to the used-car business and uses transparency as a competitive advantage.

In the world of insurance, Progressive has attained its competitive advantage by showing what competitors charge, even when Progressive isn't the cheapest option.

3. CARMAX: WHAT THEY DON'T KNOW WILL HURT US!

While the new car purchasing process is open and efficient, for used-car buyers things haven't changed much. On most car lots, haggling is required, the true state of the car is unknown, and the value of the trade-in varies greatly. Most consumers dread the whole process.

Carmax has capitalized on this frustration by leaving nothing hidden. When customers log on to the company's Web site (www.carmax.com) and specify their location, they can see the price of any car. They can look at vehicles side by side, with photos, comparing everything from a list of options to miles per gallon. Financing estimates, reviews from independent car sites, and insurance quotes are all available from the Web site.

When visiting the lot, consumers find a very different operation than they're used to seeing. The price is posted on every car. The company states, "All sales consultants are paid the same, no matter which car you buy." Associates carefully explain how Carmax certifies its vehicles, even using a demo vehicle to illustrate problems customers should be watching for when they buy a used car.

If a customer has a car to sell, Carmax will provide a written statement on what they will pay, regardless of whether a customer buys a vehicle from them or not.

The company guarantees in writing that the mileage on the odometer is correct and that no flood damage has occurred. They assure customers that a checklist of over 100 points must be passed before a vehicle is allowed on the lot. As additional assurance, after a customer buys a vehicle, a 5-day money-back guarantee is in place and customers automatically receive a 30-day warranty. Carmax offers in-house financing, but allows customers 3 days to find a better deal on their own, with no penalty.

For service, prices for most jobs are clearly posted in the service area. The company will apply these prices to any car, whether purchased from Carmax or not.

The results:

- Carmax has a Web site just for happy customer testimonials, at www.IloveCarmax.com. Every week they receive more submissions.

- Despite having only 43 retail locations in 21 markets, Carmax sold its one millionth vehicle only 10 years after it opened its first lot.

- Recent annual sales have topped $4 billion, and annual profits are over $100 million. Store sales are growing 6 to 8 percent annually, despite a recent recession and perpetual no-interest financing specials on new cars.

4. PROGRESSIVE INSURANCE: TRANSPARENCY IS IN SIGHT

If ever there was an industry where consumers could really use some help in price shopping, it would be insurance. Before the advent of the Internet, insurance buyers would either spend hours on the phone doing price comparisons with agents, or would just take their chances with one agent, not knowing if they were being overcharged or not.

Consumers still need to shop around, but one company is not afraid to show how they stack up. Progressive Insurance not only provides price shoppers with a quote on their own policy but they also provide quotes for many of their major competitors. A person who contacts Progressive or fills in information on their Web site will immediately see how Progressive stacks up against competitors.

What's more, anyone who logs on to www.Progressive.com can see a scrolling list of quote comparisons entered by *other* potential customers. In many cases, Progressive is not the cheapest quote. Sometimes they're the clear winner, but other times they're not even close. So why show the bad along with the good?

Results:

- Progressive placed fifth in a recent *BusinessWeek 50* ranking of best-performing large public corporations from the Standard & Poor's 500 index.
- For many years, Progessive's Web site has won awards from Gomez (www.gomez.com), including "Best Site for Auto Insurance Buyers" and "#1 Insurance Web Site for Ease of Use."
- Progressive placed fourth in a recent *Barron's 500* ranking of company performance for investors.
- Quarterly profits are averaging about $250 million and annual premiums written are increasing in excess of 25 percent. During the recession between early 2000 and mid-2003, Progressive's stock price doubled.

BEING TRANSPARENT *AND* MAKING MONEY

As each of these four case studies illustrate, transparency is not a cost to the bottom line, but a supercharger for the top line. But no organization can wave a wand and become magically more transparent. Commitment from the top, understanding and support throughout, internal technologies, training programs, and people policies that encourage integrity must all be in place. Even those used as examples in this book have room for improvement.

Achieving transparency that pays real dividends requires a moral compass and a well-thought-out road map. This entire book is dedicated to making the case for that compass. The final chapter suggests some processes for creating the map.

TRANSPARENCY IN ACTION:

STRATEGY AND EXECUTION

Honesty and transparency make you vulnerable.
Be honest and transparent anyway.

—MOTHER TERESA

Trust, then verify.

—RONALD REAGAN

Creating a transparent organization requires a broad combination of attitudes and attributes:

- An appropriate culture
- Establishment of far-reaching policies and practices
- Sophisticated training
- Programs and processes to protect competitive intelligence
- Open support for those who demonstrate integrity in all their endeavors and censure for those who don't
- Active two-way communication between important stakeholders

Such things don't happen quickly or easily. They take time and hard work. They require consistency through management transitions and industry upheavals. While best-practice efforts can increase revenues on the top line and pay dividends at the bottom line, they often call for significant monetary and human resource expenditures over long periods of time and throughout the organization. World-class organizations know that the transparency ground rules are changing. Therefore, they are taking the lead in creating strategies that alter the competitive landscape of their industries. They are not only adopting transparency best practices but they are also making transparency a distinctive competency that generates real market value for their organizations.

TRANSPARENCY: CHANGING AN INDUSTRY'S RULES OF ENGAGEMENT

Business books offer various definitions and approaches to strategy. Most of them are helpful in coping with new transparency demands. For our purposes, the following definition is offered:

> *Strategy* is the process of understanding an industry's structure and dynamics, determining the organization's relative position in that industry, and taking action to improve results by either changing the industry's structure or the organization's competitive position.

While changing an industry's structure might seem like an impossible task, several small (at the time) companies have done just that over the past several decades: Wal-Mart, Southwest Airlines, Charles Schwab, eBay, and Dell. Each used different means to change the industry, but in each case *they remade their industry on terms most favorable to themselves.*

As Chapter 7 described, BP, Chile, Carmax, and Progressive Insurance are using transparency, at least in part, to do the same. They are ahead of all their peers in changing the rules of engagement in their respective areas. Competitors, ultimately, have to follow. But the leaders chart the path, arrive first, and reap most of the rewards.

Not all organizations can or should adopt industry-altering strategies. But every organization has the opportunity to embrace transparency and make it a distinctive competency within their organization to create real stakeholder value.

TRANSPARENCY: DISTINCTIVE ORGANIZATIONAL COMPETENCY

Organizations are constantly confronted with challenge and change. To deal with it in a coherent way, the following framework called *The Five A's of Strategic Planning* is a useful guide. The five steps are Strategic *Audit*, Strategic *Analysis* (Internal and External), Strategic *Assessment*, Strategic *Alternatives*, and Strategic *Action*.

A complete exploration of this process is beyond the scope of this book. A brief look at each step, however, is presented to assist organizations to develop a transparency strategy and action plan:

1. TRANSPARENCY: A STRATEGIC AUDIT

Management scholar David Baron suggests a four-part analysis for the audit of nonmarket factors such as transparency: Issue, Interests, Institutions, and Information.

ISSUES

- Growing global public consensus demands and ever cheaper and more powerful technologies deliver greater transparency in every aspect of the organization.
- Availability of such information whets the public appetite for more.
- The Information-Transparency Cycle grows ever more powerful.

INTERESTS

Demand for more transparency is expected from a wider array of stakeholders, including:

- *Shareholders (donors, voters, membership, and so forth).*
  Shareholders are challenging more corporate actions, staging
  proxy fights, and subscribing to in-depth rating services. They
  are flexing their muscles in shareholder meetings or voting
  with their feet by selling shares or pulling donations.

- *Employees.* There will be increasing pressure for more
  information on every aspect of the organization's policies
  from hard-to-find, skilled, and mobile employees. The
  pressure increases as demographic factors force a skilled
  labor shortage in the coming decades.

- *Watchdogs and special interest groups.* Assume the organization
  is being closely watched, ranked, and rated on a variety of
  measures. Some groups are positive, some neutral, while
  others passionately espouse ideas that further their own
  agendas.

- *The media.* Large, fragmented, multifaceted, and powerful
  media organizations compete to get the inside scoop, but
  unite to get the full story. The Internet greatly expands
  news outlets and instantly makes any news global.

INSTITUTIONS

More institutions claim stakeholder status, including:

- *Regulatory agencies.* The SEC, FDA, EPA, FTC, and OSHA
  are under public pressure themselves to take decisive
  actions. Their action imperative is to "protect the public
  interest," regardless of the organizations or economic consequences.

- *City, state, and federal lawmakers.* Politicians, like regulators,
  are under fire for their own transparency issues, and skillfully
  shift the media and public glare elsewhere. Not to be
  dismissed lightly, they hold the key to new laws and
  prosecution.

- *Trade associations and self-governing bodies.* Expect these groups
  to cheerlead, set standards, guide and police their members

- *Unions.* Faced with dwindling members and reasons to exist, unions take up the task of forcing corporate transparency as a means of creating new sources of value to members.

- *International governance and trade organizations.* These groups grow stronger daily and set the ultimate standards for all organizations.

INFORMATION

Demand for new depth in and kinds of information grows unabated:

- *Internal information.* New regulations require establishment of internal audits and regular reviews of risk management. Teams, budgets, metrics, processes, and standards are needed. Internal auditors over time are charged with more than financial processes and include all areas of potential risk.

- *External reporting.* Demands for more, better, faster financial reporting continue unabated. New lines of quantitative and qualitative inquiry are related to organizational value drivers such as the organization's long-term goals or missions and progress toward achievement; impacts of macro and micro economic climate; market share data; human resource metrics such as compensation policies and workplace diversity, labor practices, workplace environment and safety; productivity indices; intellectual property valuations; R&D, innovation, or improvement process results; customer satisfaction results; environmental impact; and political and charitable contributions.

2. TRANSPARENCY: A STRATEGIC ANALYSIS

- *Internal analysis.* Every organization needs to carefully assess its strengths and weaknesses in systematically gathering and analyzing information to meet or exceed its specific transparency demands. Assessment is required of the capabilities required to tune in to the evolving agendas of various groups (watchdog groups, special interest groups, employees, and so forth) to see where future pressures are likely to arise.

- *External analysis.* This involves a careful analysis of external forces and their apparent power to shape transparency demands that create organizational opportunities or threats.

While no list could be comprehensive enough to cover every organization, the following are general observations:

- Forces for increased transparency grow stronger every quarter, with the expectations coming from all angles, both internal and external.
- The free fall in the cost of information will continue to provide both the demand for and means to achieve total transparency.
- The types of transparency demanded progress from the financial to the nonfinancial and encompass virtually all areas of organizational activity.
- Transparency becomes a key component of every organization's operating and reporting activities.
- The demand for internal transparency equals or exceeds that of external transparency.
- New metrics are derived to grade the adequacy and comparability of an organization's transparency within and across industries.

3. TRANSPARENCY: A STRATEGIC ASSESSMENT

Strategic assessment involves making a determination of the organization's position relative to others in its strategic set and best-in-class organizations from any sector. PricewaterhouseCoopers,

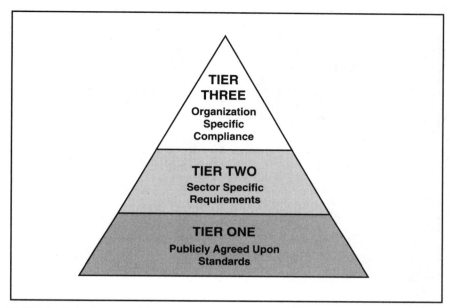

FIGURE 8.1   Strategic Transparency Assessment.

in their report on corporate transparency, proposed a useful model in this regard (see Figure 8.1). The model is adapted to accommodate more than public corporations. At the bottom are broad public requirements on reporting (for public companies, such things as GAAP rules). In the center are industry-specific metrics and standards for industry comparison. At the top is a range of organization-specific information such as strategy, compensation, corporate governance, and risk management.

4. TRANSPARENCY: STRATEGIC ALTERNATIVES

Following an in-depth analysis of an organization's internal and external realities regarding transparency and a careful assessment of an organization's relative position in terms of its industry and the general public environment, it needs to adopt a

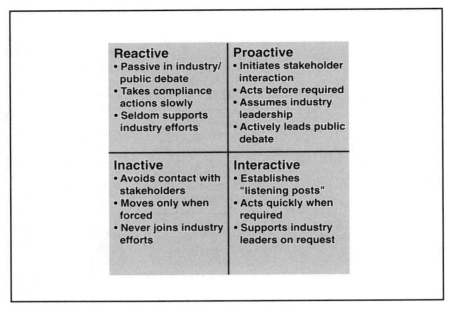

FIGURE 8.2   Alternative Organizational Strategies for Transparency.

strategy from the four basic approaches depicted in Figure 8.2. This figure illustrates the strategy and the main execution characteristics of each approach.

5. TRANSPARENCY: STRATEGIC ACTION PLAN

Once a specific strategy is selected, execution aspects need to be addressed. At a minimum, they include:

- Board of Directors' statement of overall policy and approach
- Board of Directors' governance programs to review progress
- Senior management articulation and promulgation of transparency strategy
- Specific, detailed, written, and widely communicated transparency practices covering the gathering, analysis, and reporting of organizational metrics

- Institutionalizing transparency as part of key employee annual objectives
- Programs for the documentation and protection of competitive assets and intelligence
- Compliance programs for routine transparency reporting
- Establishment of future transparency analysis and monitoring teams
- Transparency training programs for employees
- Engagement programs to encourage customer, partner, supplier participation, and support
- Programs to recognize and reward exemplary performance
- Whistleblower programs
- Communication programs for key stakeholders
- Establishment of feedback channels
- Evaluation programs to monitor progress
- Contingency plans to prepare for routine but unforeseen events or requests
- Crisis management plans to deal with major catastrophes

ESTABLISHING WHISTLEBLOWER PROGRAMS

The Sarbanes-Oxley Act of 2002 created greater legal protection for whistle-blowers and mandated that policies be institutionalized within public companies. Although only publicly traded companies must comply, organizations of all kinds need to seriously consider adopting such plans. Best practice would include, at a minimum:

- A clear policy of protection for those reporting fraud or cover-ups

- A clearly defined channel for reporting, preferably through multiple internal and external channels, without requiring notice to the person's manager

- Written guidelines on how reports will be investigated and what actions will be taken if wrongdoing is uncovered

- A written statement that every effort will be made to keep concerns confidential

KEEP YOUR EYES ON THE PRIZE

Transparency is nothing if not about seeing things more clearly. To many, demands from outsiders for more transparency about private or corporate actions and intentions seem intrusive and ill-placed. In some cases, they're right.

But in the main, transparency's promise is a better world for all. This book doesn't need to make that case, history already has.

What the book attempts, instead, is to alert readers to the *new* transparency: what it is and how it's changing; why the demand for it is unstoppable; who's watching whom, and why; what to expect in the future; and how to act on, and strive for, compliance.

But being transparent, really transparent, is not for the faint of heart. It takes guts and determination. And it probably won't happen without challenges from both inside and outside the organization. Athletes, in the middle of their epic battles for supremacy in some team sports, often get discouraged about the ups and downs, aches and pains, agonies of defeats, and the setbacks from injuries. The winners though have an expression: Keep your eyes on the prize.

Transparency is no different. Despite the difficulties, achieving transparency brings real rewards for the winners.

RESOURCES

U.S. GOVERNMENT AGENCIES

Department of Health and Human Services
http://www.hhs.gov/

Department of Labor (DOL)
http://www.dol.gov/

Environmental Protection Agency (EPA)
http://www.epa.gov/

Federal Election Commission (FEC)
http://www.fec.gov/

Federal Trade Commission (FTC)
http://www.ftc.gov/

Food and Drug Administration (FDA)
http://www.fda.gov/

Securities and Exchange Commission (SEC)
http://www.sec.gov/

U.S. General Accounting Office (GAO)
http://www.gao.gov/

FINANCIAL REPORTING

Accountancy Age
http://www.accountancyage.com/

American Institute of Certified Public Accountants
http://www.aicpa.org

Financial Accounting Standards Board
http://www.fasb.org/

International Accounting Standards Board
http://www.iasb.org.uk

Public Company Accounting Oversight Board
http://www.pcaobus.org/

FINANCIAL EVALUATION

Standard & Poors
http://www.standardandpoors.com

Standard & Poors Governance Services
http://www.governance.standardandpoors.com

Moody's
http://www.moodys.com

Morningstar
http://www.morningstar.com/

Value Line
http://www.valueline.com/

Sanford C. Bernstein & Co.
http://www.bernstein.com

Investor's Business Daily
http://www.investors.com/

SUSTAINABILITY REPORTING

Global Reporting Initiative
http://www.globalreporting.org/

SocialFunds.com
http://www.socialfunds.com/

CorpWatch
http://www.corpwatch.org/

"BIG FOUR" AUDITING FIRMS

PricewaterhouseCoopers
http://www.pwc.com/

KPMG
http://www.kpmg.com

Deloitte Touche Tohmatsu
http://www.deloitte.com

Ernst & Young
http://www.ey.com

WATCHDOG ORGANIZATIONS
HUMAN RIGHTS AND GOVERNMENT CORRUPTION

Amnesty International
http://www.amnesty.org/

Fair Labor Association
http://www.fairlabor.org/

Global Exchange
http://www.globalexchange.org/

Lawyer's Committee for Human Rights
http://www.lchr.org/

Transparency International
http://www.transparency.org/

Publish What You Pay
http://www.publishwhatyoupay.org/index.html

Human Rights Watch
http://www.hrw.org/

International Labor Rights Fund
http://www.laborrights.org/

International Labour Organization
http://www.ilo.org/

BUSINESS PRACTICES AND PRODUCTS

Business in the Community
www.BITC.org/

Better Business Bureau
http://www.bbb.org/

Consumer Reports
http://www.consumerreports.org

Consumer Voice USA
http://www.consumervoiceusa.com

National Consumers League
http://www.nclnet.org/

Weiss Ratings
http://www.weissratings.com/

SHAREHOLDER RIGHTS

Shareholder Action Network
http://www.shareholderaction.org/index.cfm

The Council of Institutional Investors
http://www.cii.org/

Institutional Shareholder Services (ISS)
http://www.issproxy.com/

Investor Responsibility Research Center
http://www.irrc.org/

PRESS FREEDOM

The Freedom Forum
http://www.freedomforum.org/

National Freedom of Information Coalition
http://www.nfoic.org/

Reporters Without Borders
http://www.rsf.org

World Press Freedom Committee
http://www.wpfc.org/index.jsp

U.S. GOVERNMENT WATCHDOGS

Common Cause
http://www.commoncause.org/

Foundation for Taxpayer and Consumer Rights
http://www.consumerwatchdog.org/

League of Women Voters
http://www.lwv.org/

Project on Government Oversight
http://www.pogo.org/

Citizens Against Government Waste
http://www.citizen.org/

National Legal and Policy Center
http://www.nlpc.org/

American Civil Liberties Union
http://www.aclu.org/

WHISTLE-BLOWING

Government Accountability Project
http://www.whistleblower.org/

Public Concern at Work
http://www.pcaw.org.uk/

National Whistleblower Center
http://www.whistleblowers.org/

NONPROFITS

Alliance for Nonprofit Management
http://www.allianceonline.org/

Better Business Bureau Wise Giving Alliance
http://www.give.org

Guidestar
http://www.guidestar.org/

International Center for Not-for-Profit Law
http://www.icnl.org

National Center for Charitable Statistics
http://nccs.urban.org/

Board Source
http://www.ncnb.org/

INTERNATIONAL INSTITUTIONS

International Monetary Fund
http://www.imf.org/

International Chamber of Commerce
http://www.iccwbo.org/

United Nations
http://www.un.org/

The World Bank
http://www.worldbank.org/

World Bank Group's Extractive Industries Review
www.eireview.org/

World Trade Organization (WTO)
http://www.wto.org/

World Economic Forum
http://www.weforum.org/

World Business Council for Sustainable Development
http://www.wbcsd.ch

DISCARDED

HF 5387 .O38 2004

Oliver, Richard W., 1946-

What is transparency